Famous Paintings
Adult Coloring Book

Sheila Dunn

About this Book

Coloring masterpieces from history is not only relaxing but wonderful practice for using color and rendering light and shadow. This book contains a sample of famous paintings selected from art history. The original painting in full color is shown on the left to provide an easy reference. However, no one should feel forced to follow the example of the original artist. Feel free to use any colors you choose.

I hope you enjoy this collection. To see original art by Sheila Dunn, please visit her Facebook artist page at www.facebook.com/Artist4Christ. On her Facebook page, you can see the latest releases of coloring books as well as what is happening in her art studio.

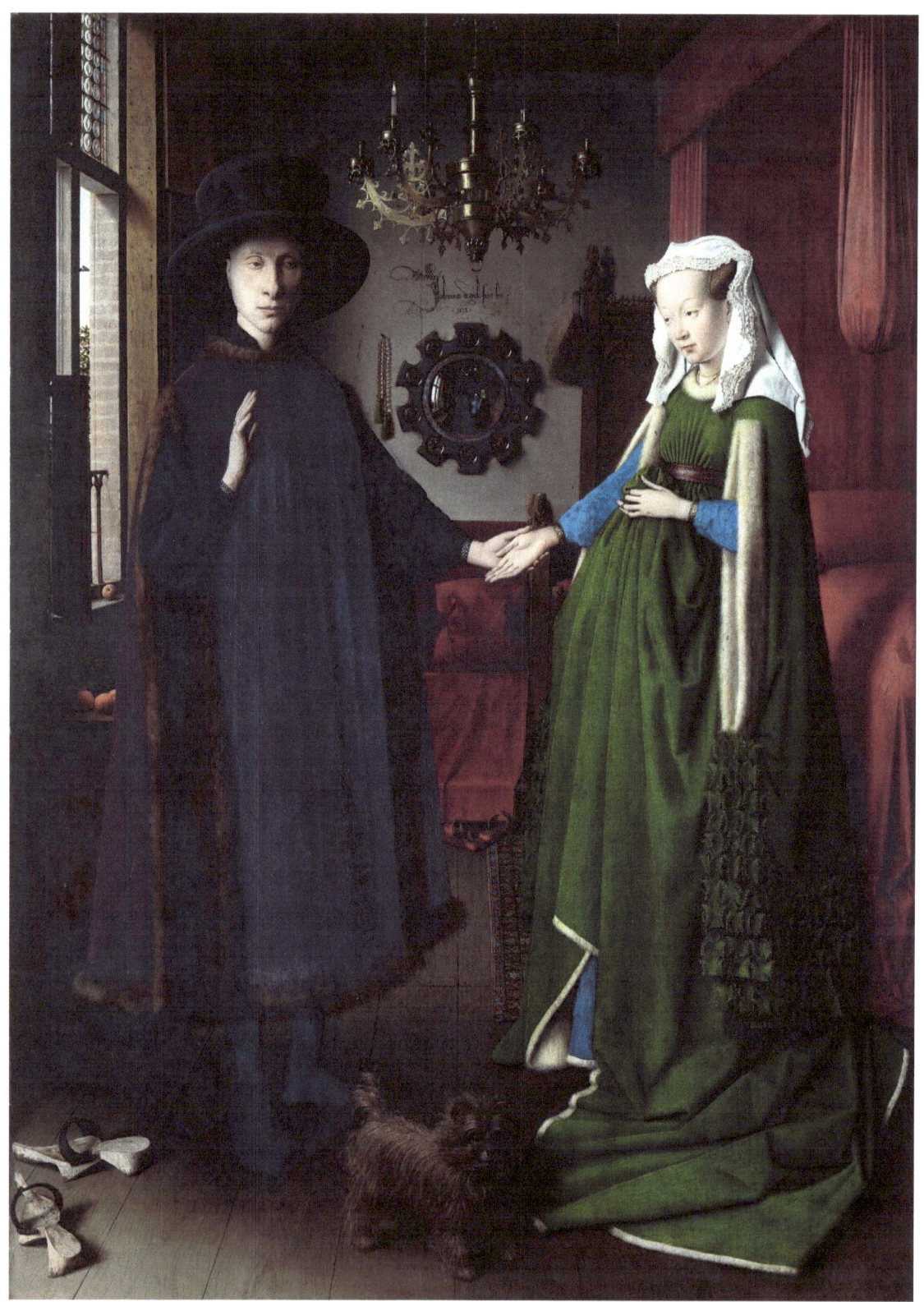

The Arnolfini Wedding (1434), Jan van Eyck

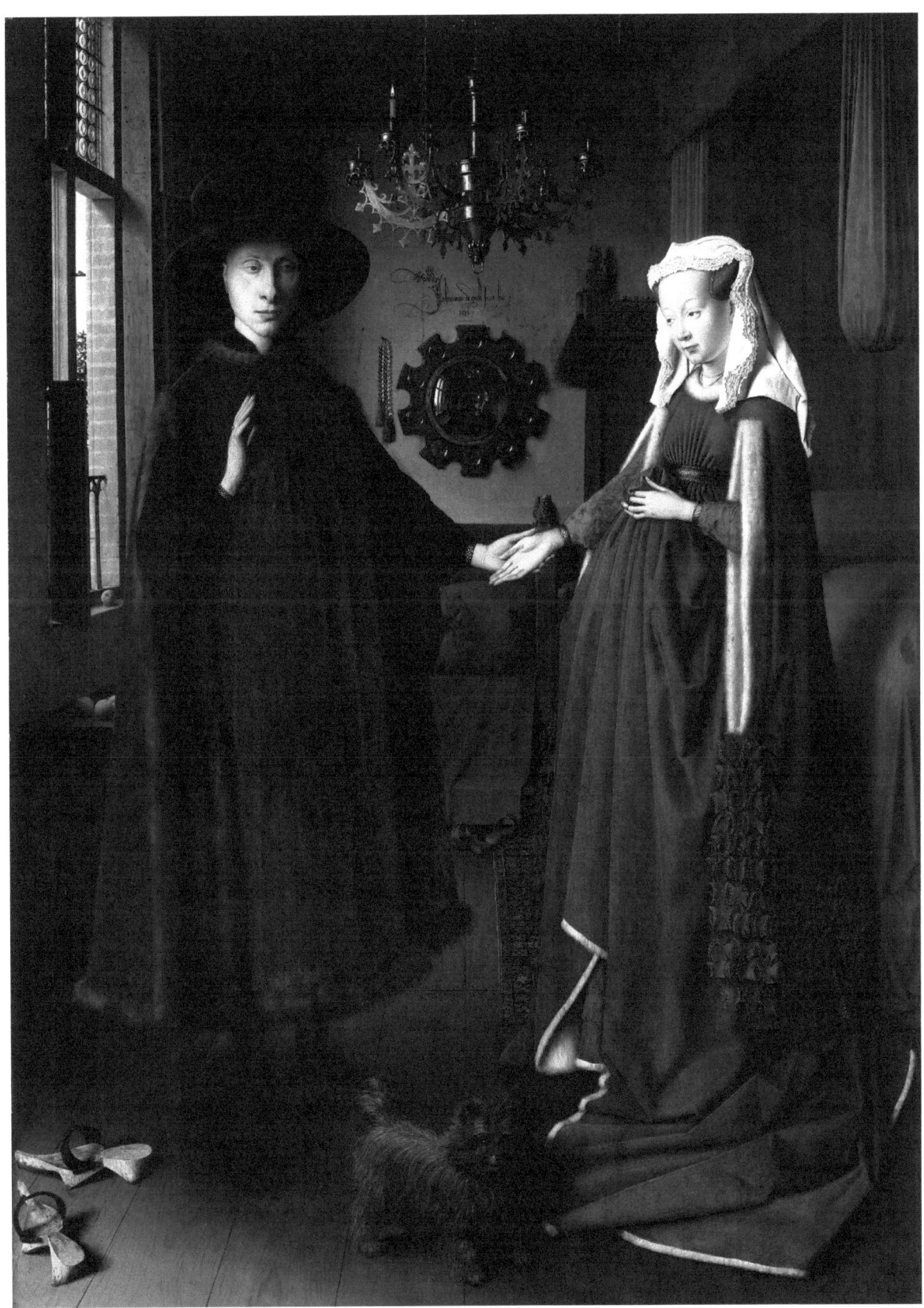

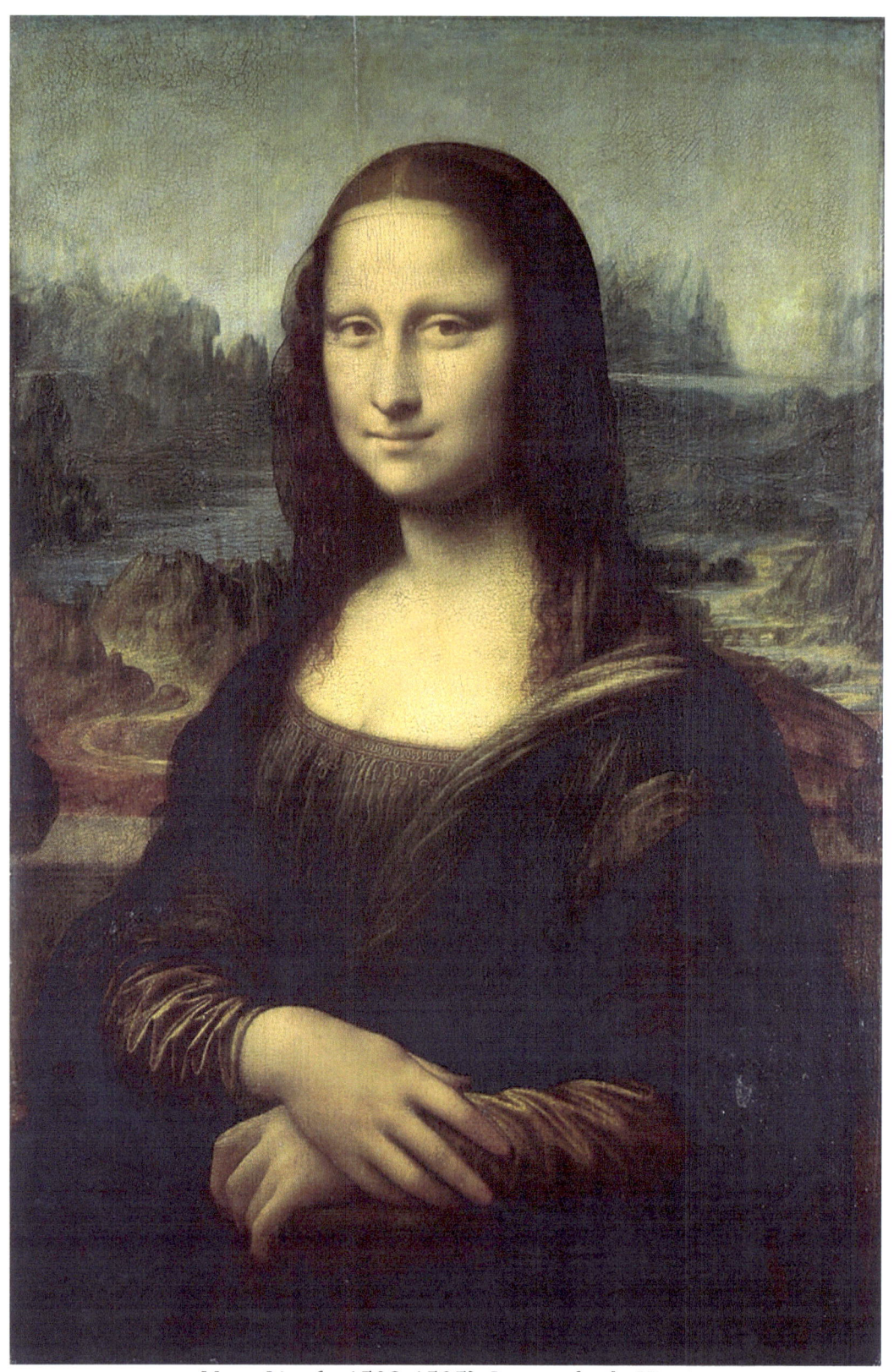

Mona Lisa (c. 1503-1505), Leonardo da Vinci

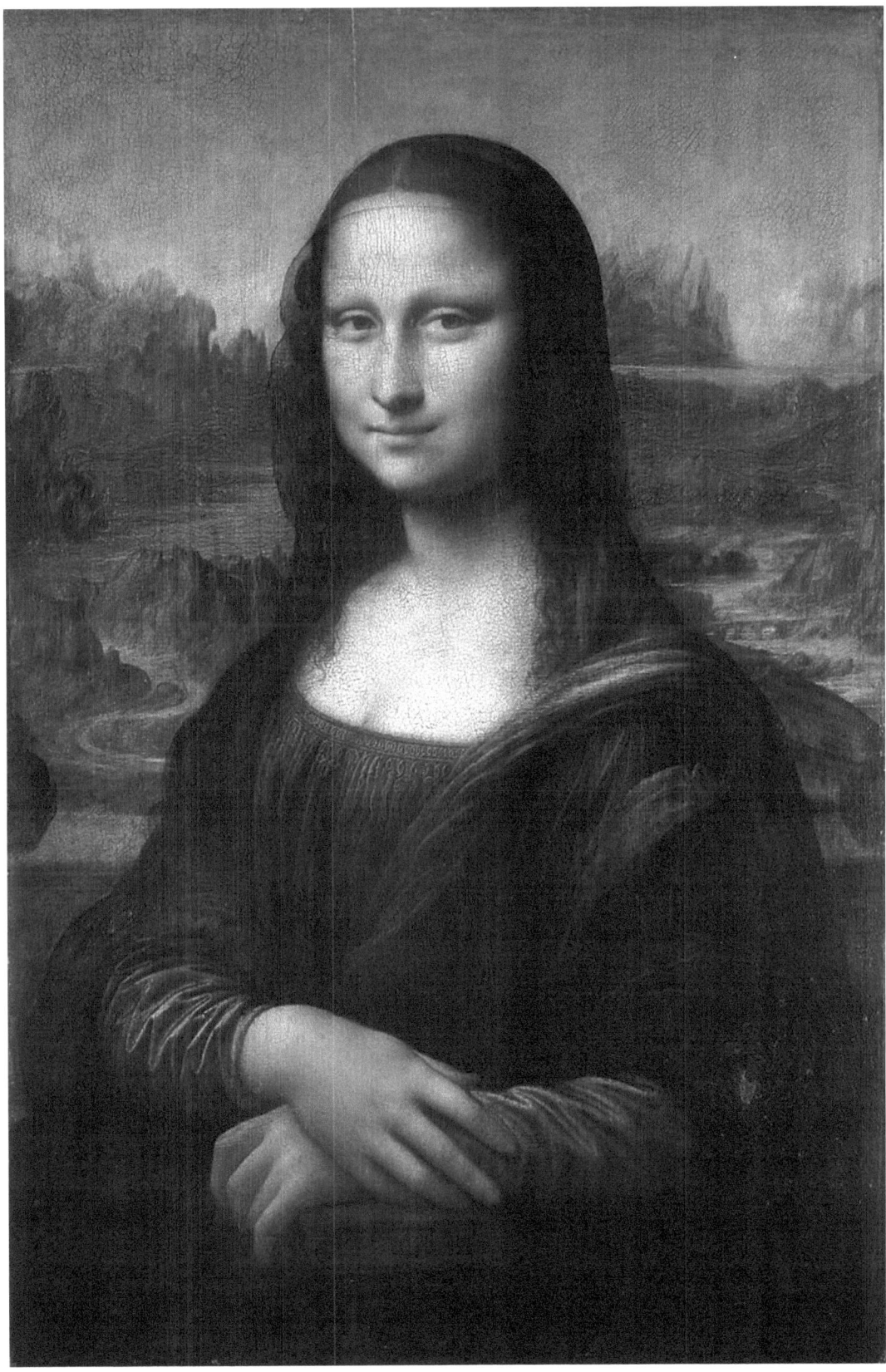

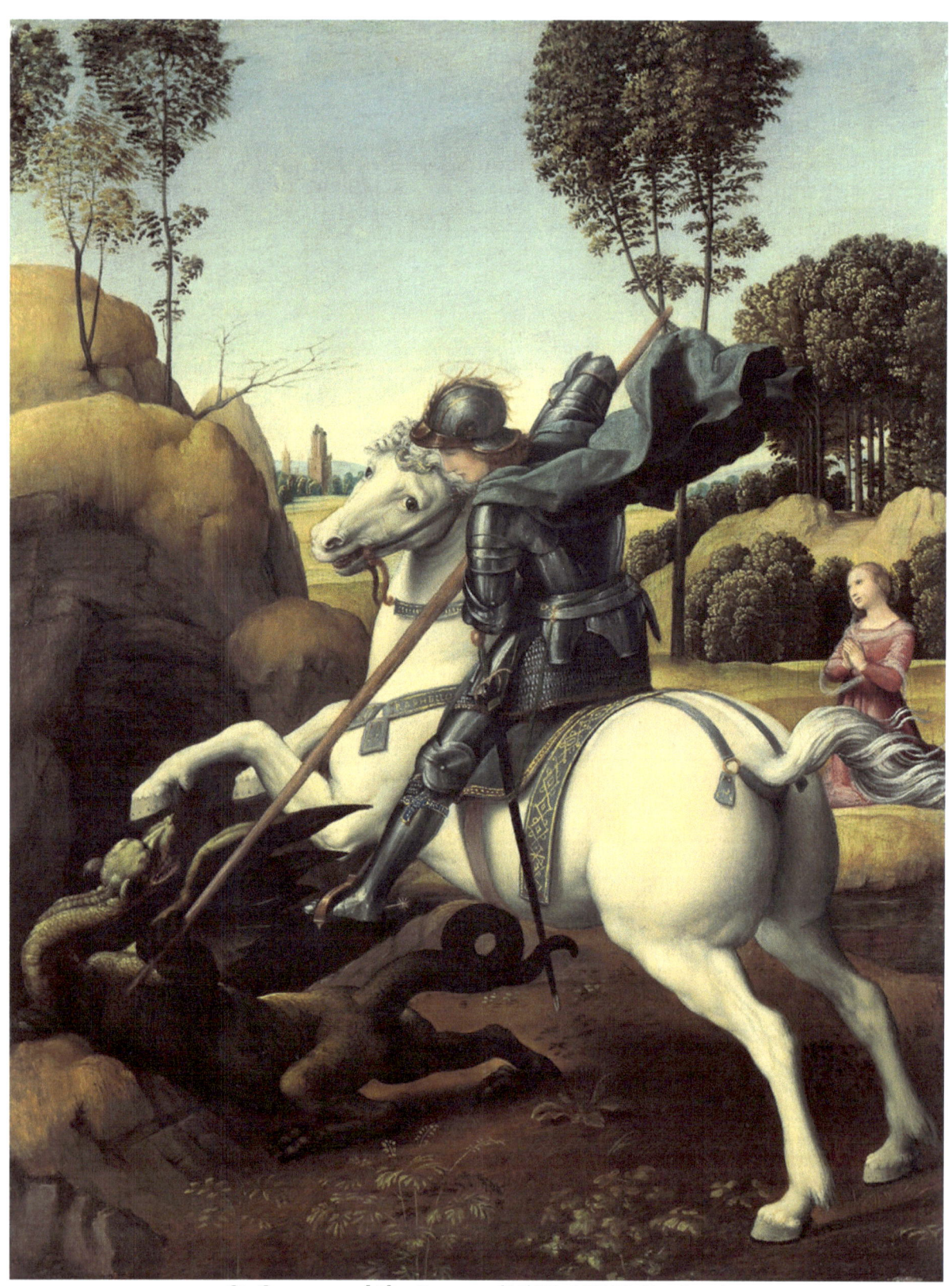

St. George and the Dragon (1505-1506), Raphael

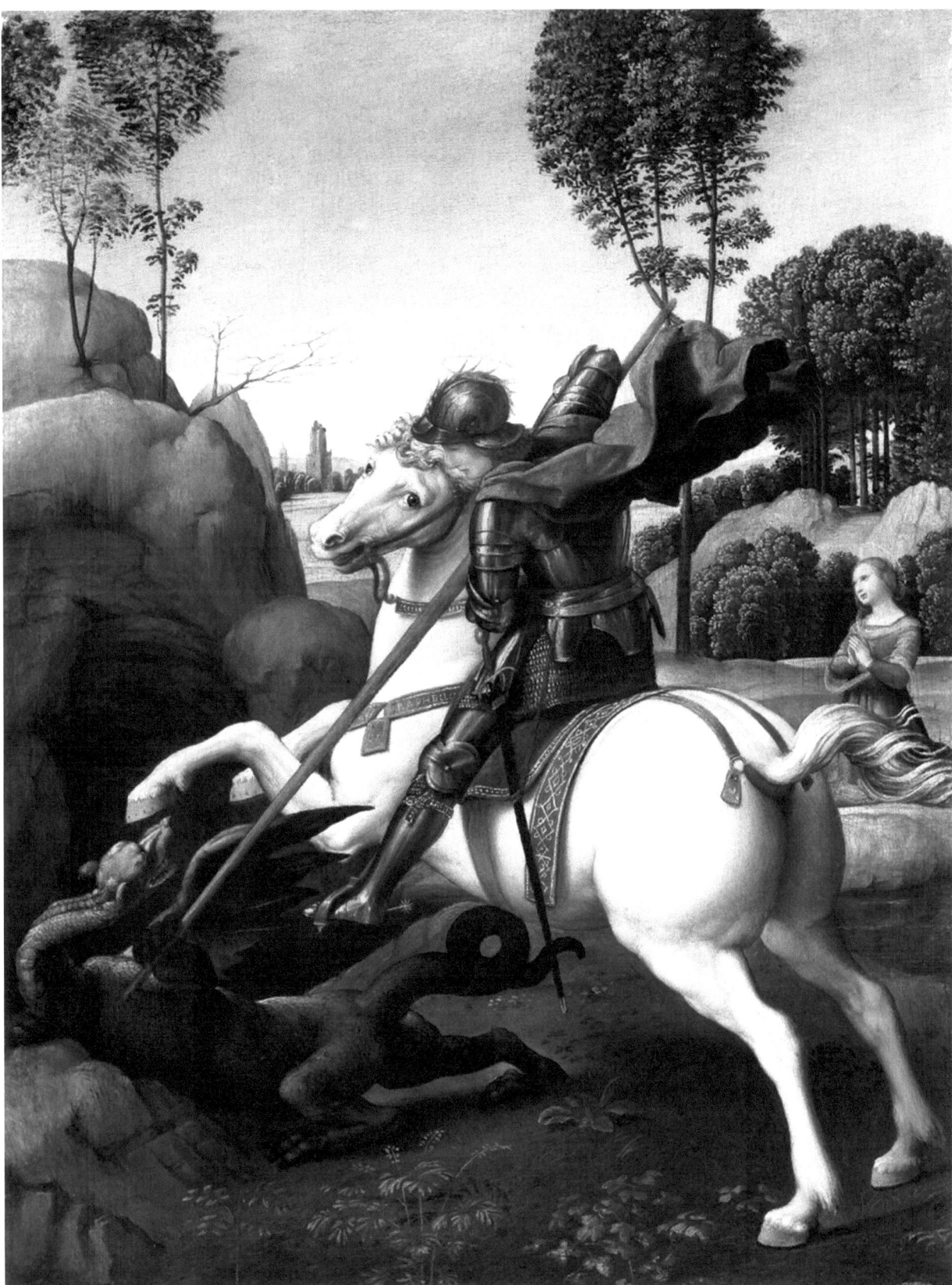

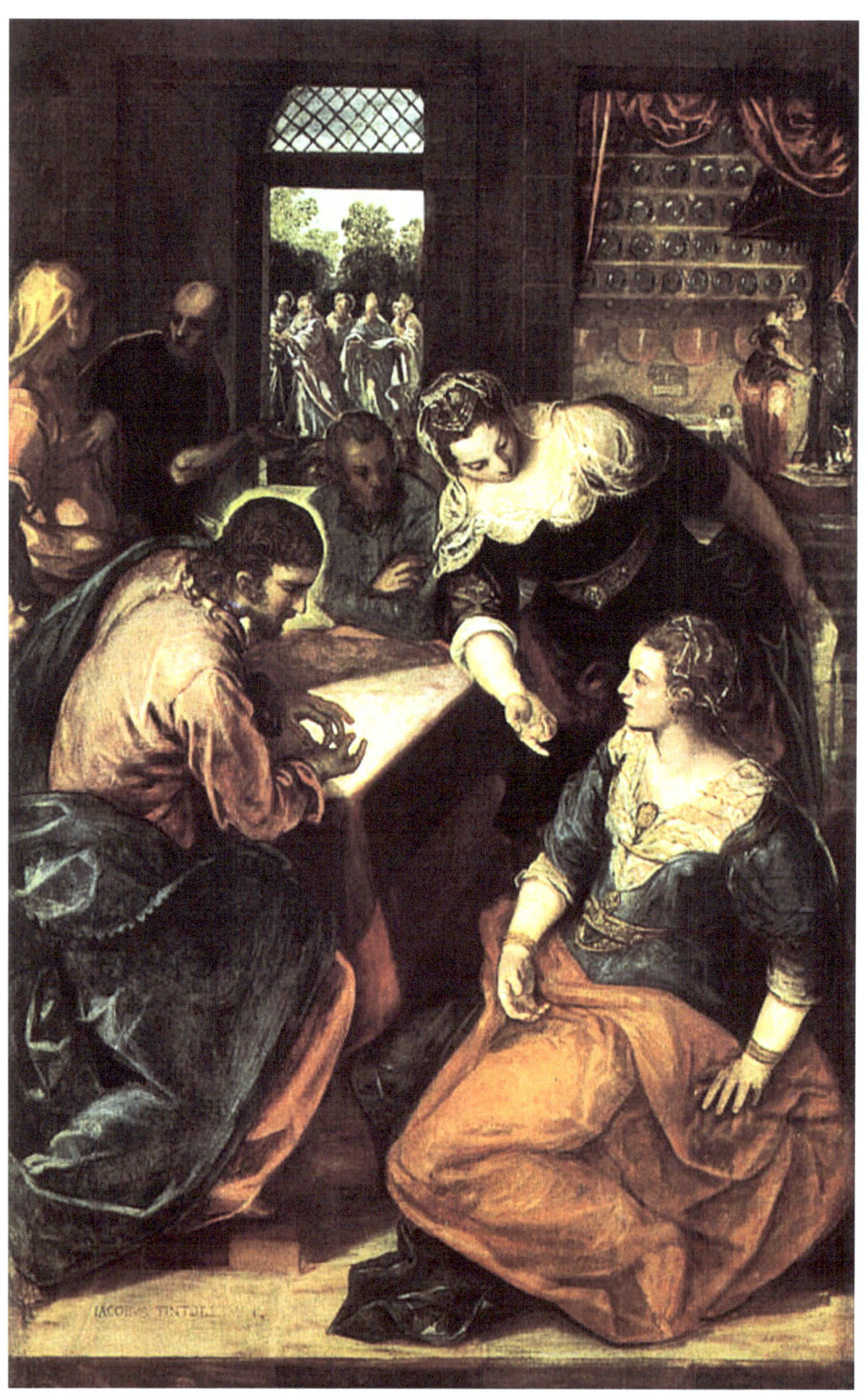

Christ with Martha and Mary (1570), Jacopo Tintoretto

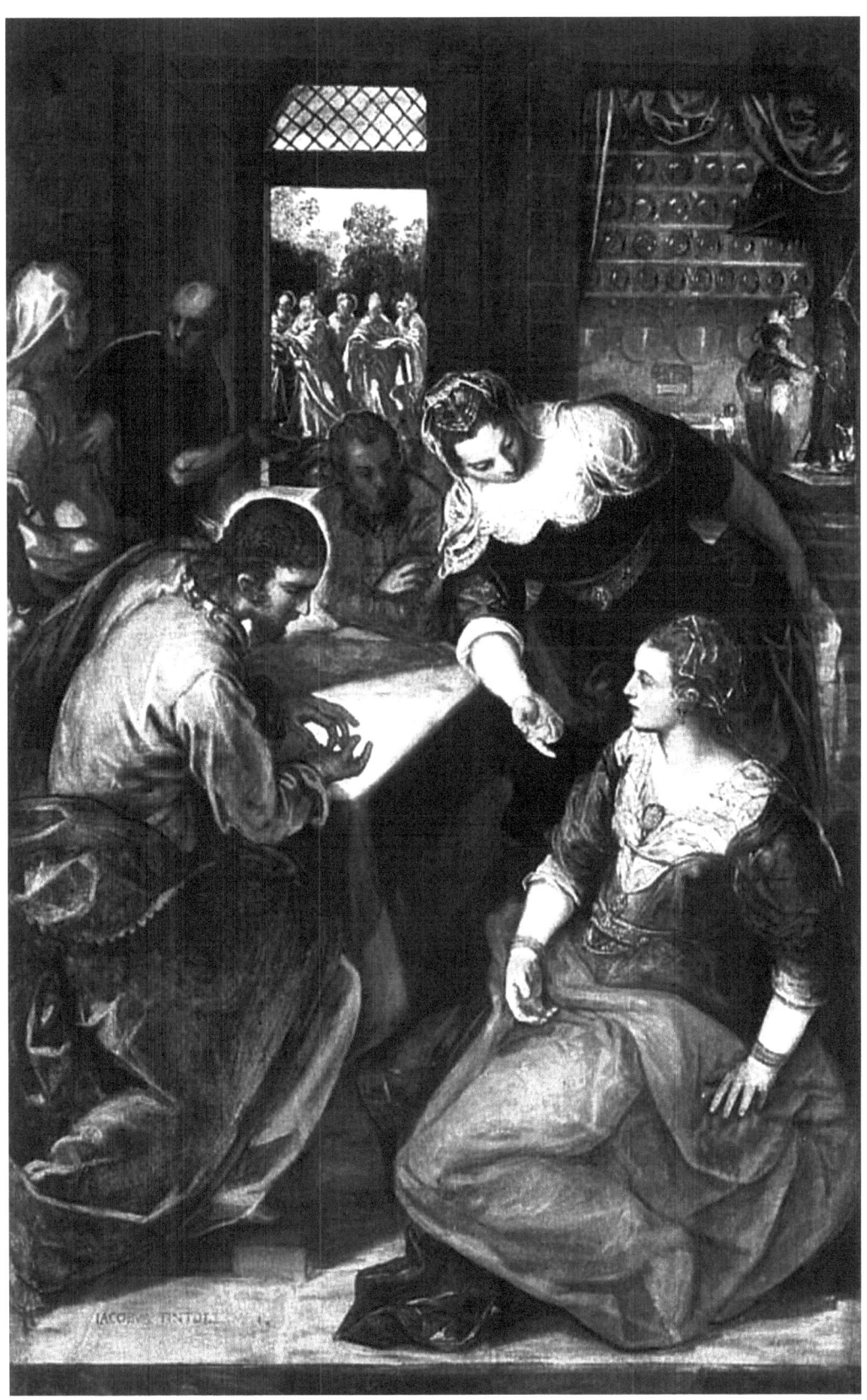

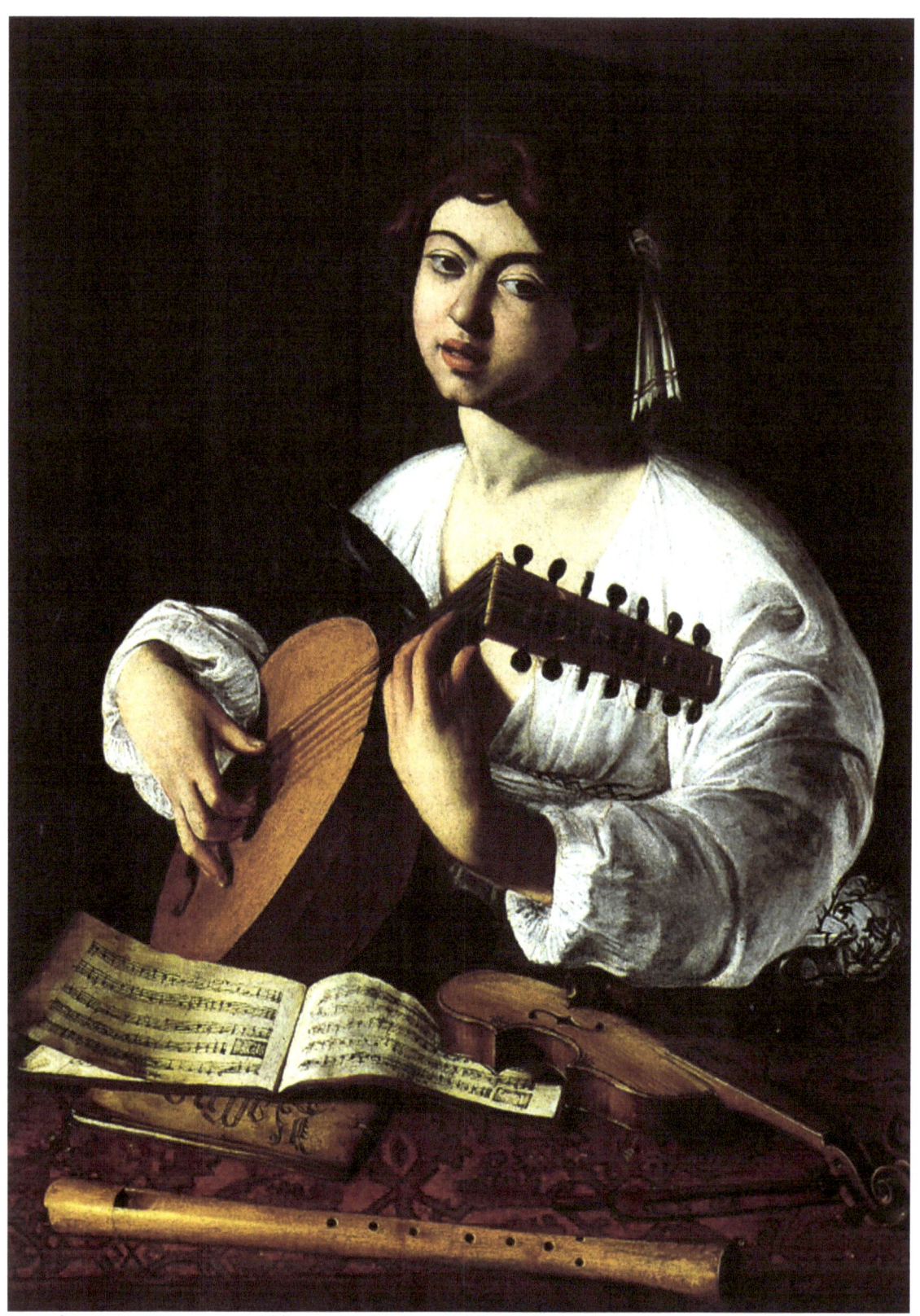

The Lute Player (1596), Caravaggio

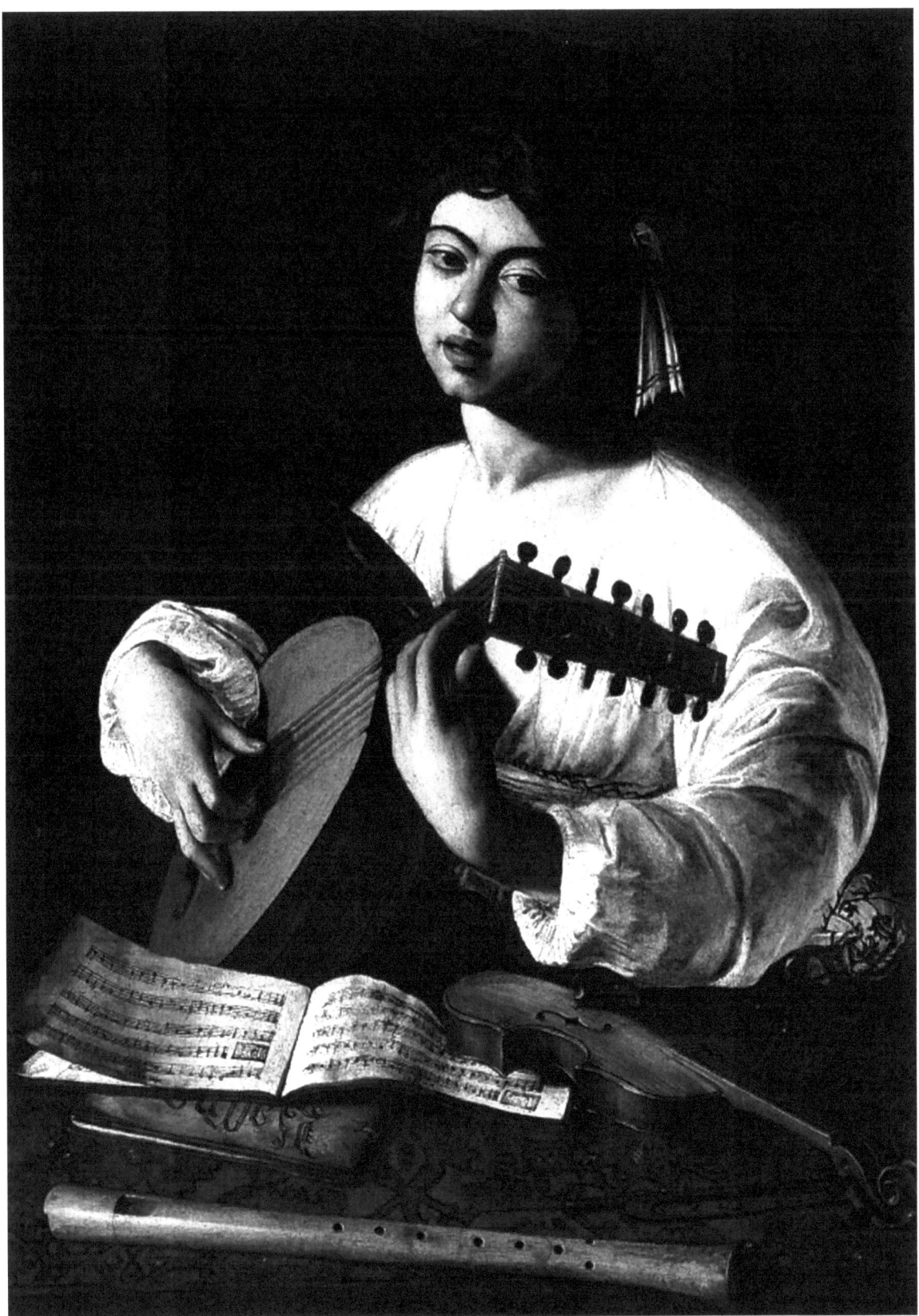

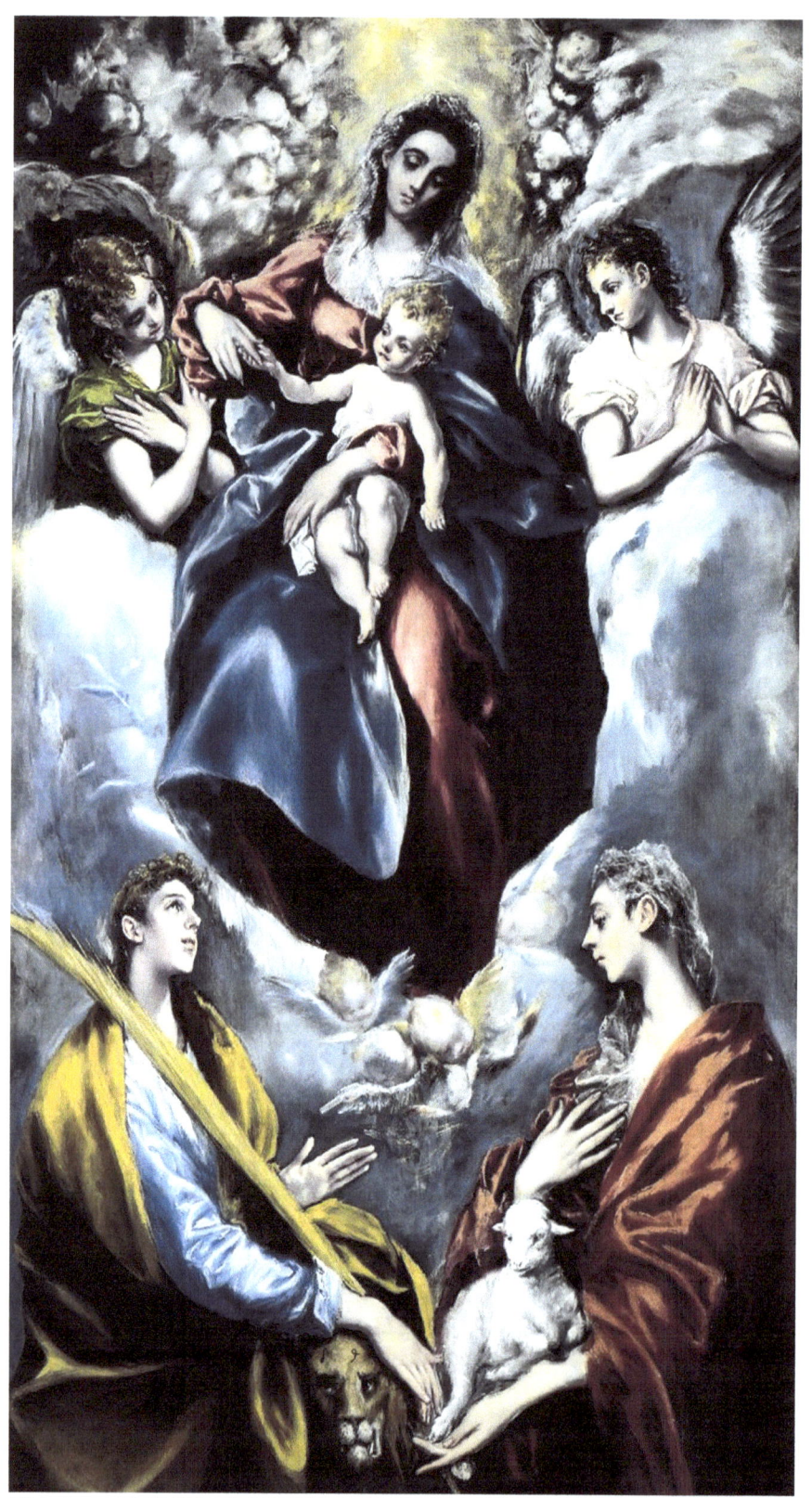

The Virgin and Child with St. Martina and St. Agnes (1597-1599), El Greco

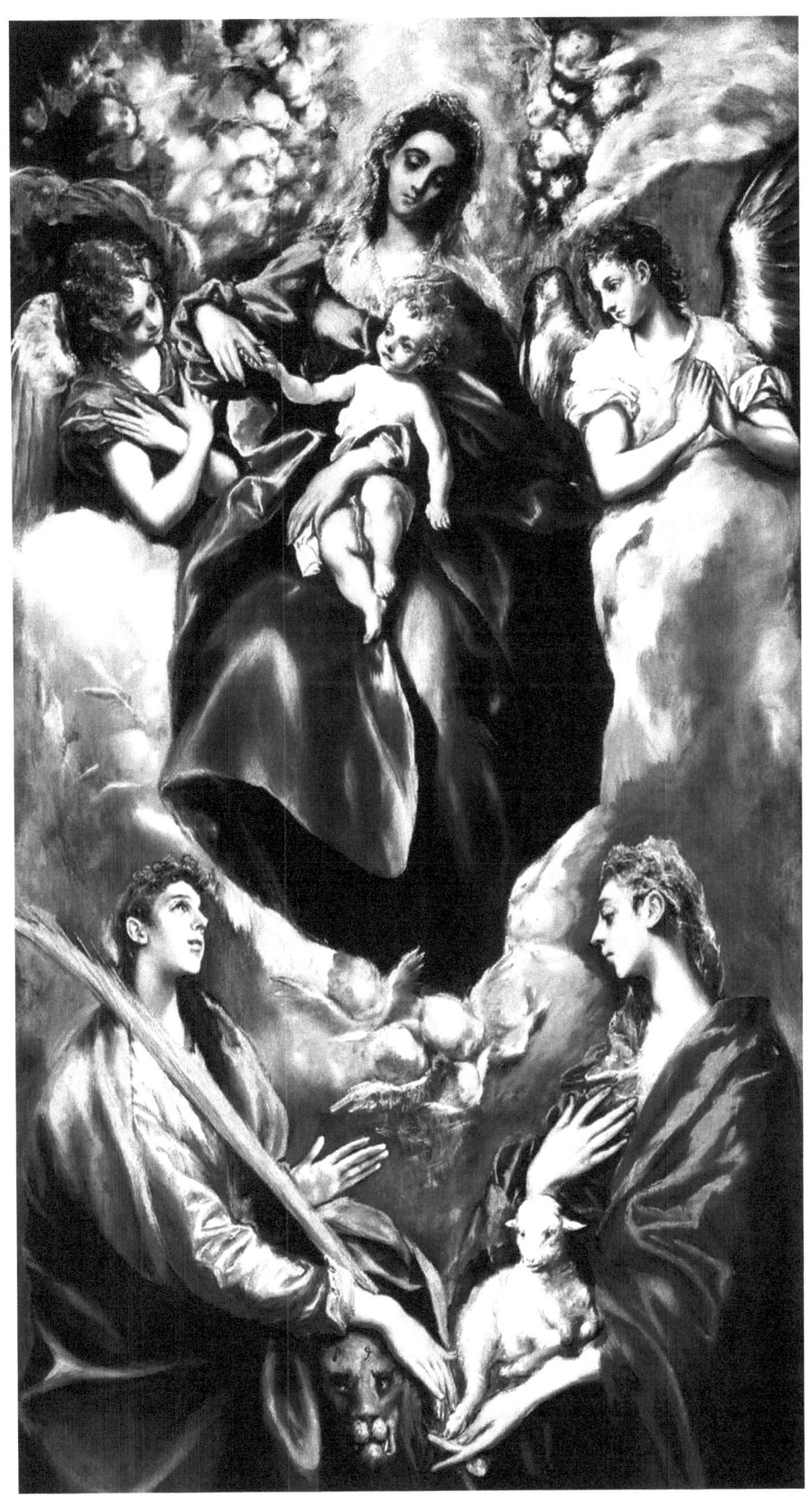

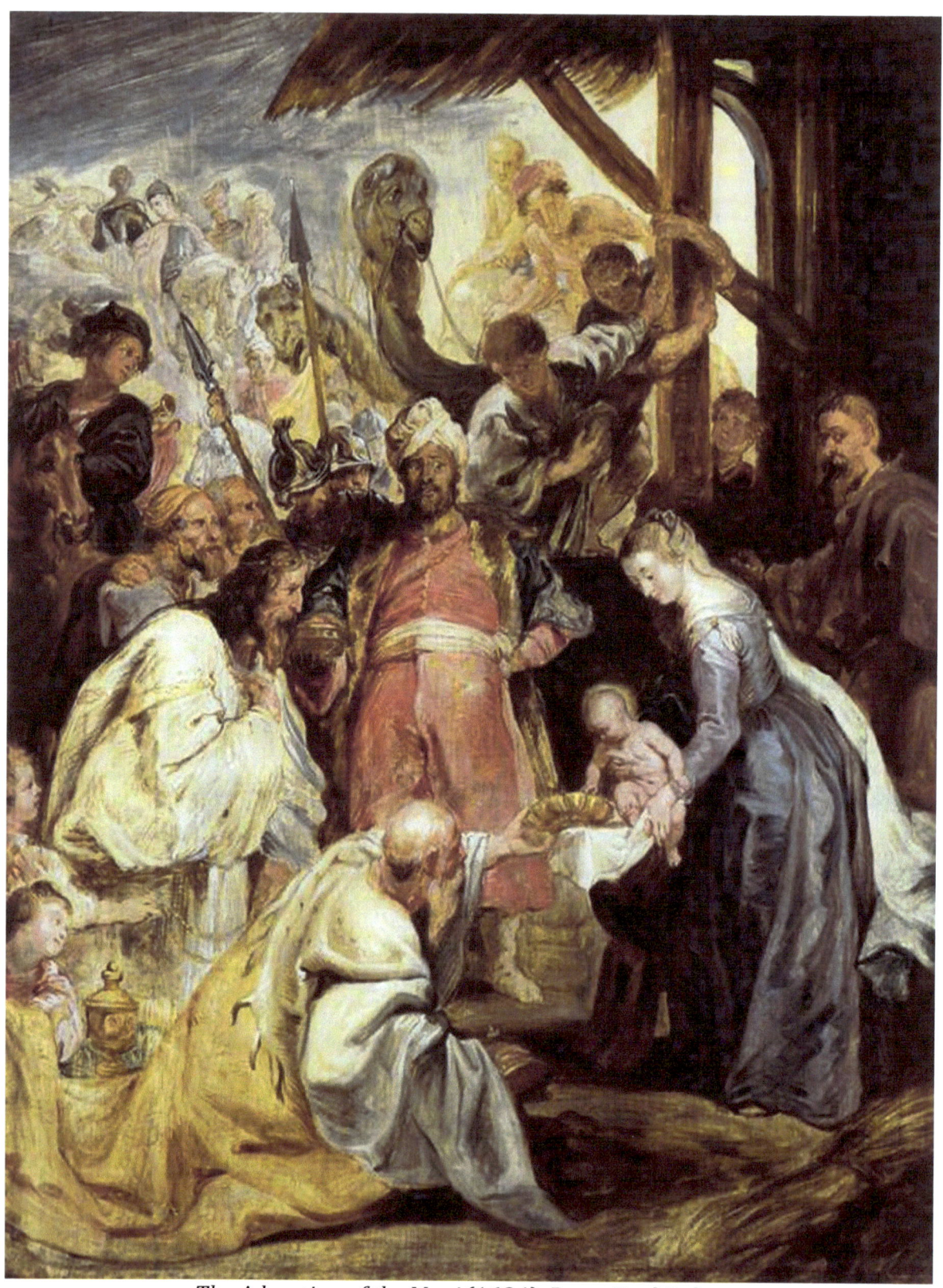

The Adoration of the Magi (1624), Peter Paul Rubens

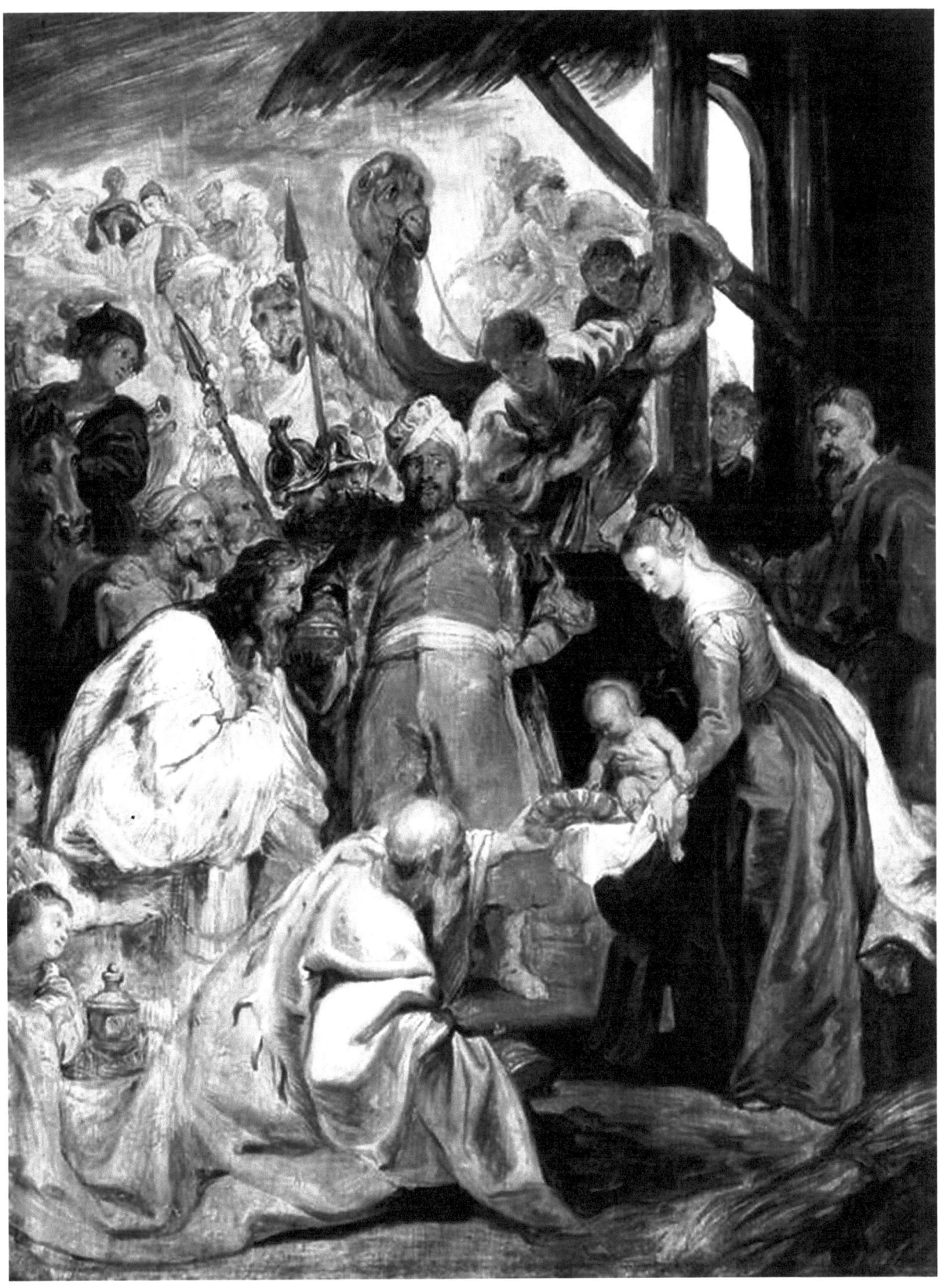

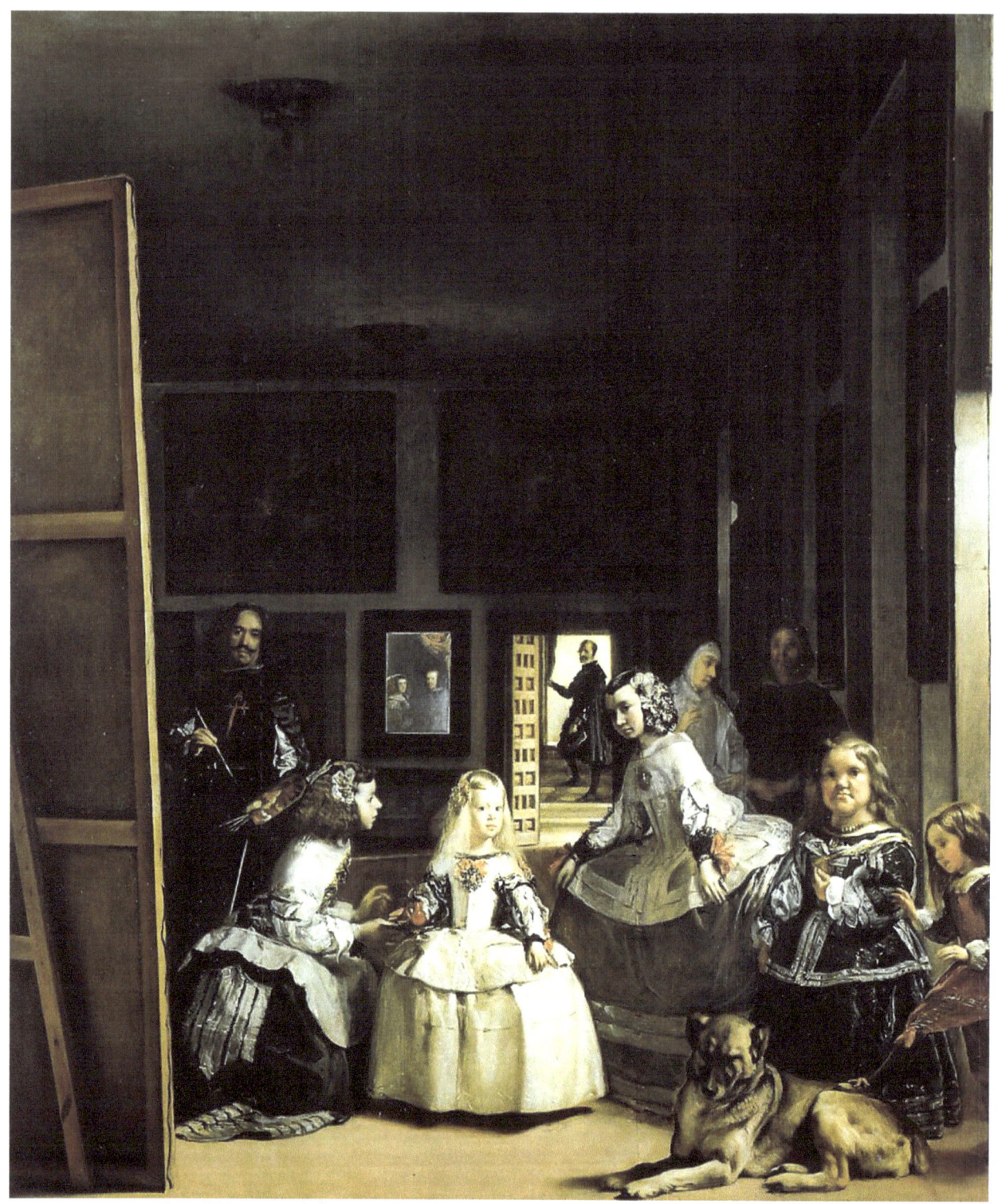

Las Meninas (The Maids of Honor) (1656-1657), Diego Velázquez

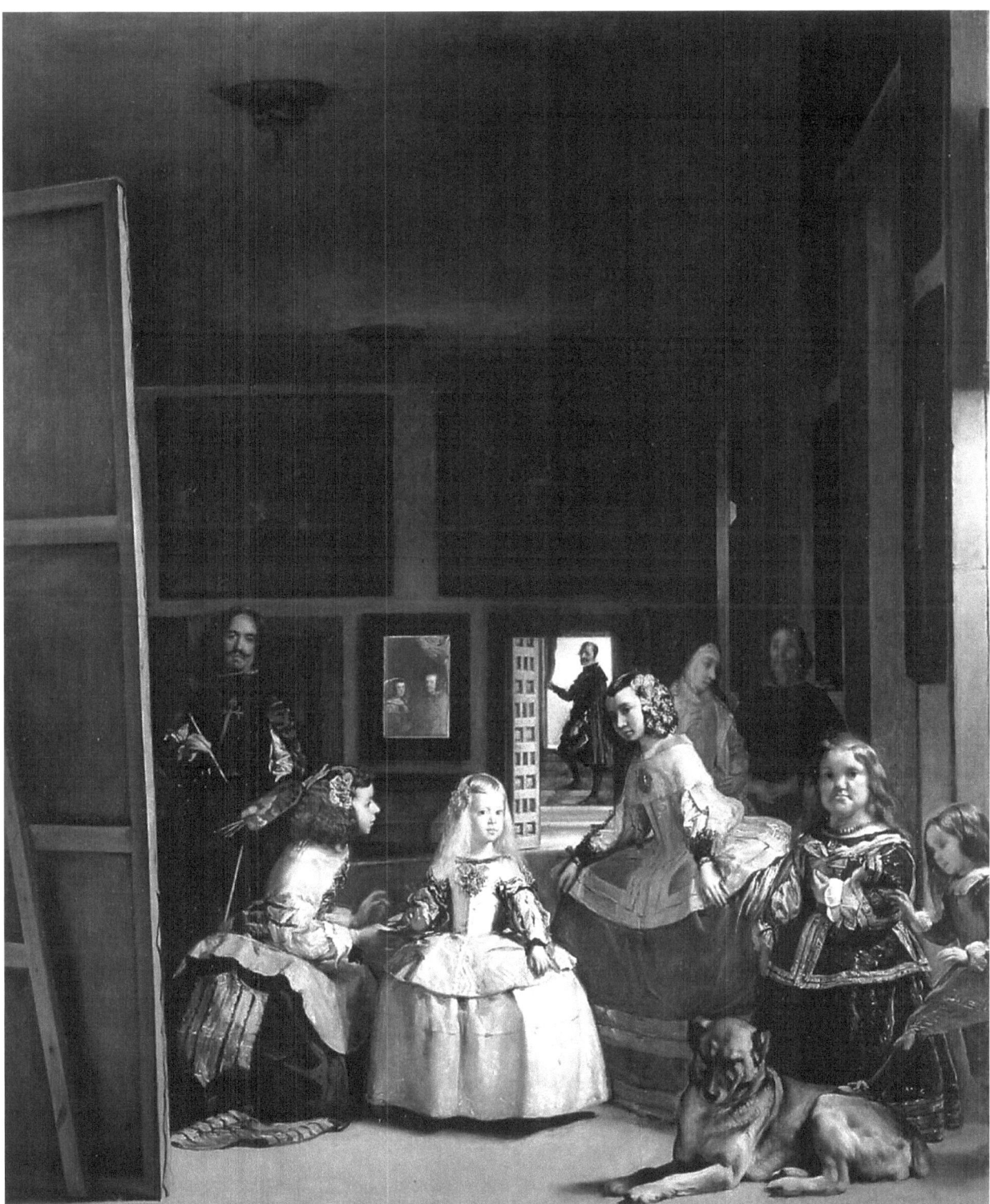

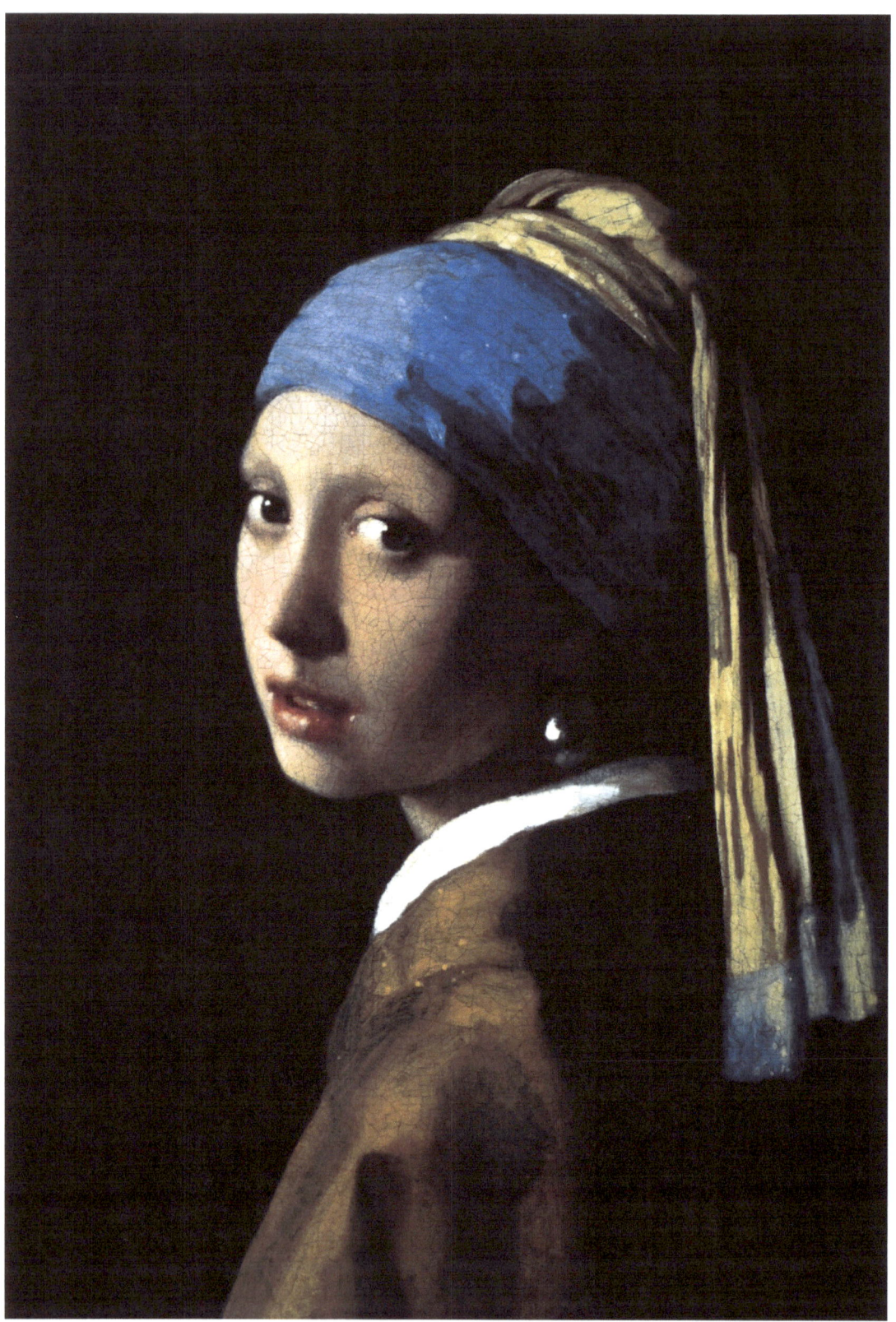

Girl with a Pearl Earring (1665-1666), Johannes Vermeer

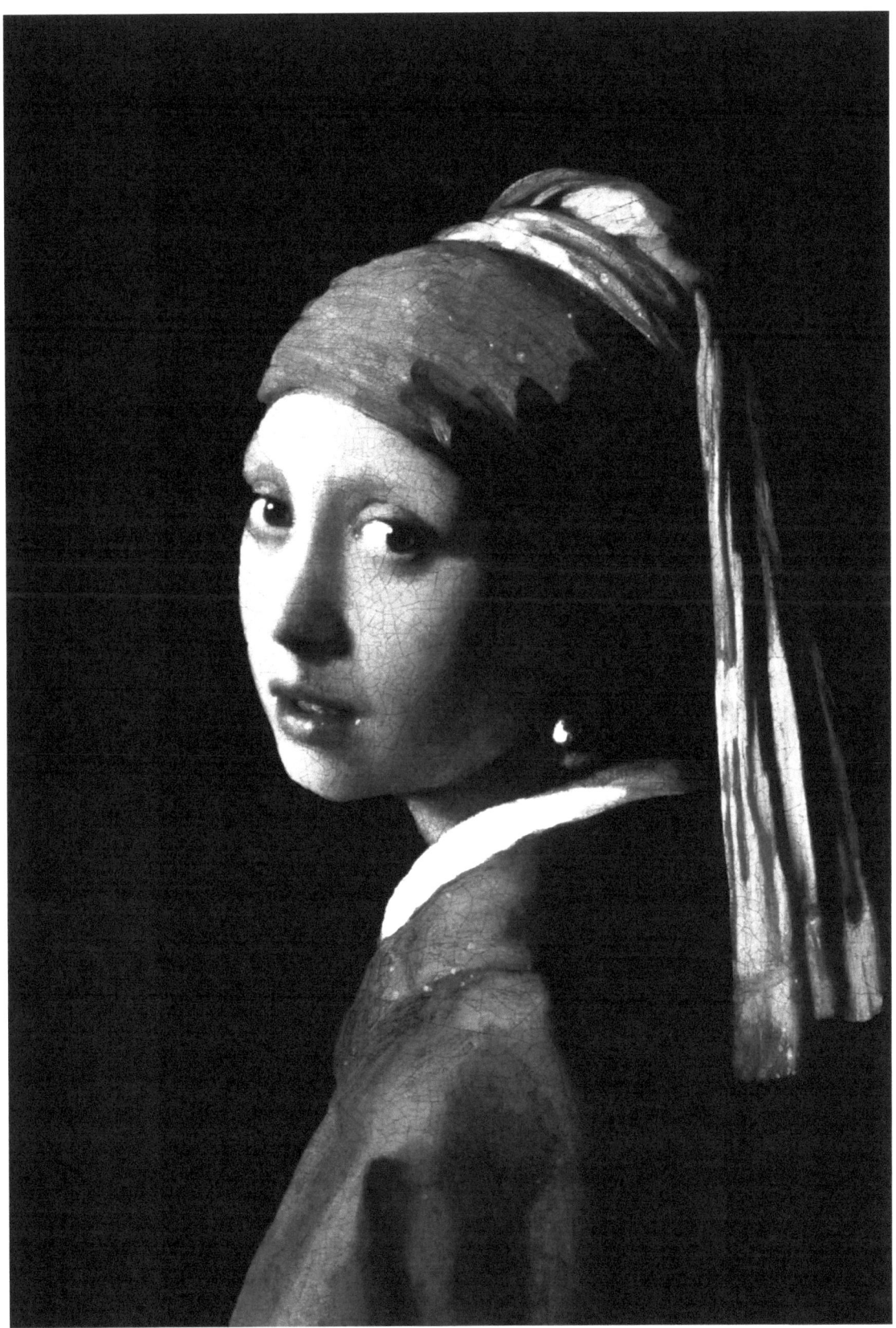

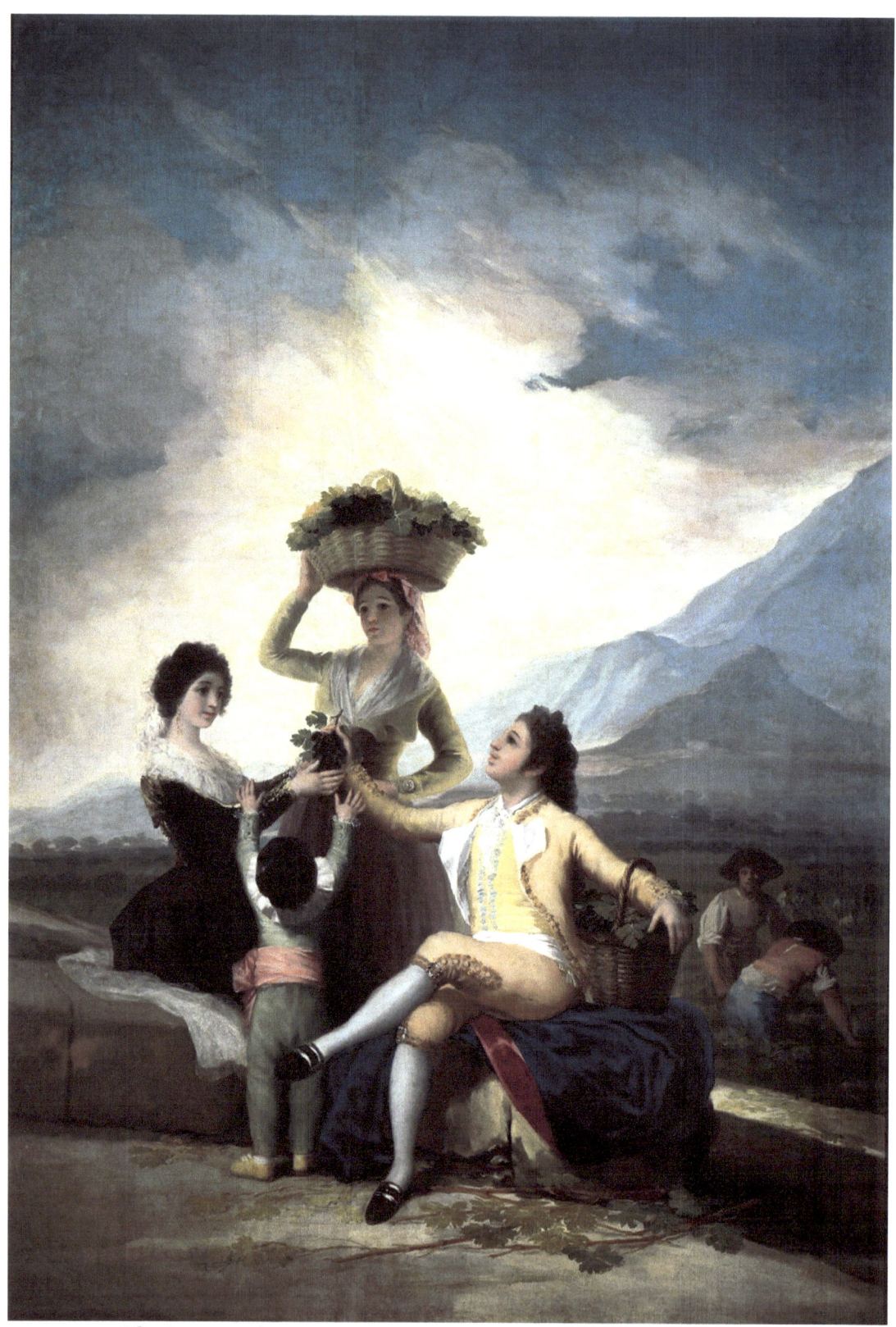

The Harvest (1786-1787), Francisco Jose de Goya y Lucientes

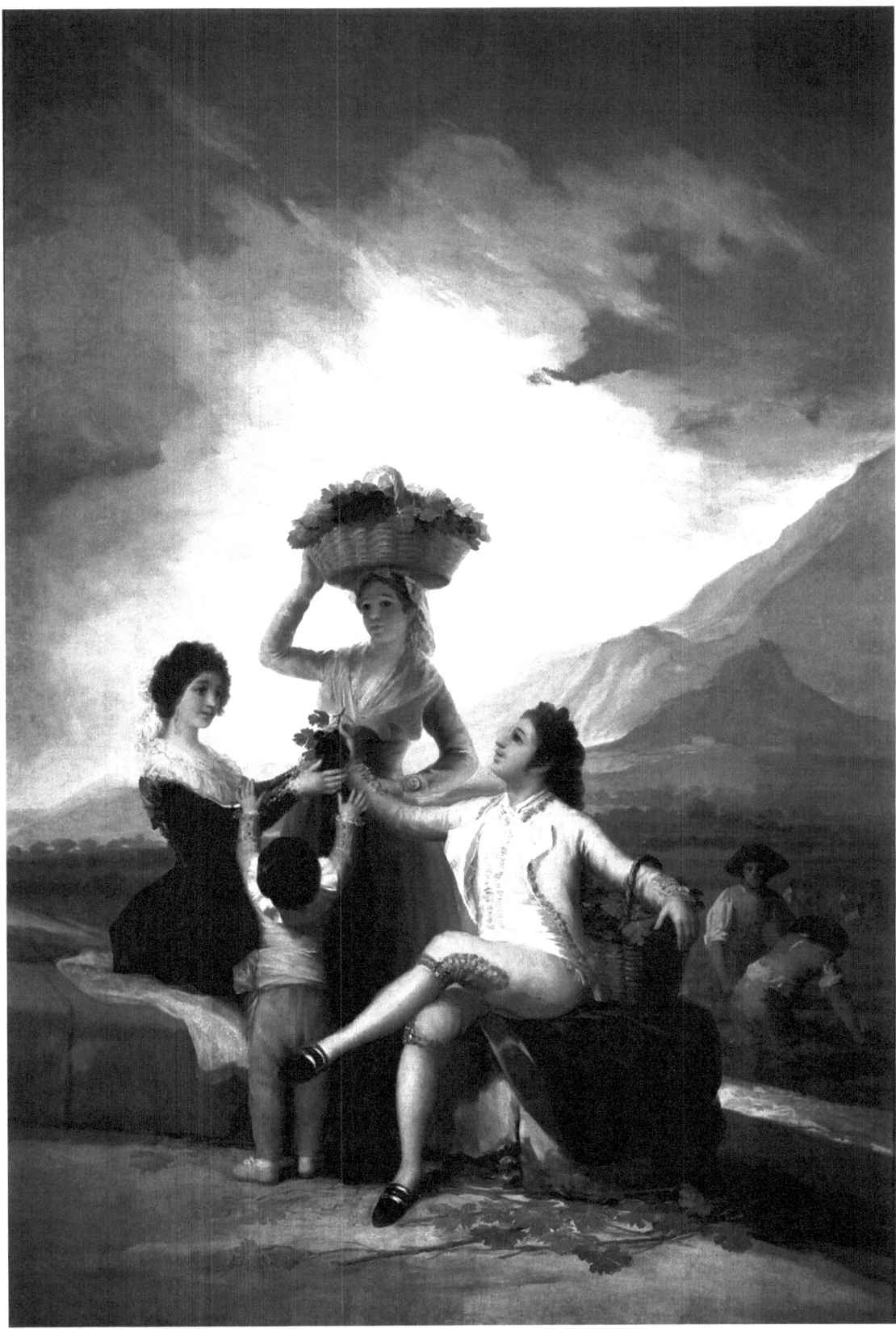

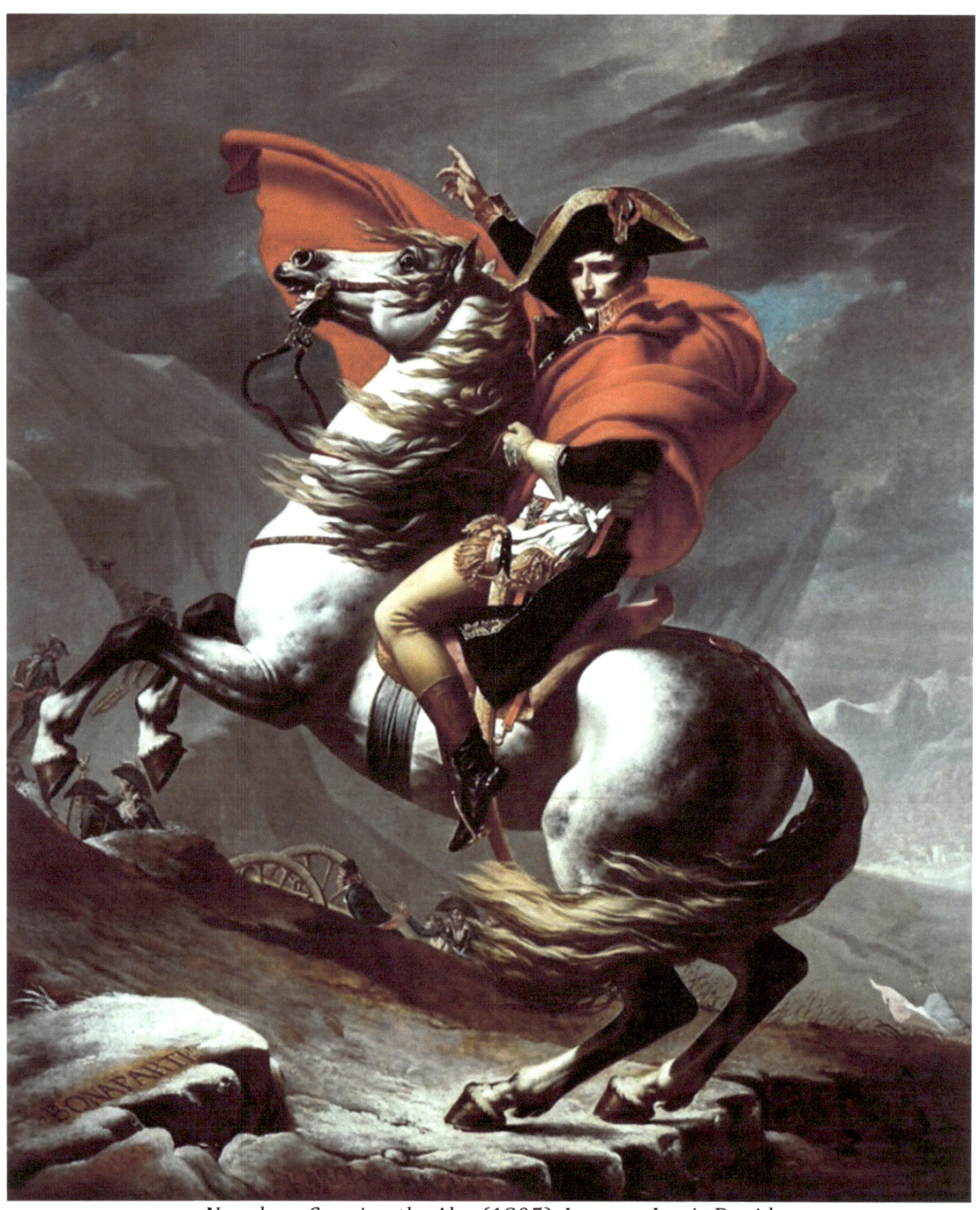

Napoleon Crossing the Alps (1805), Jacques-Louis David

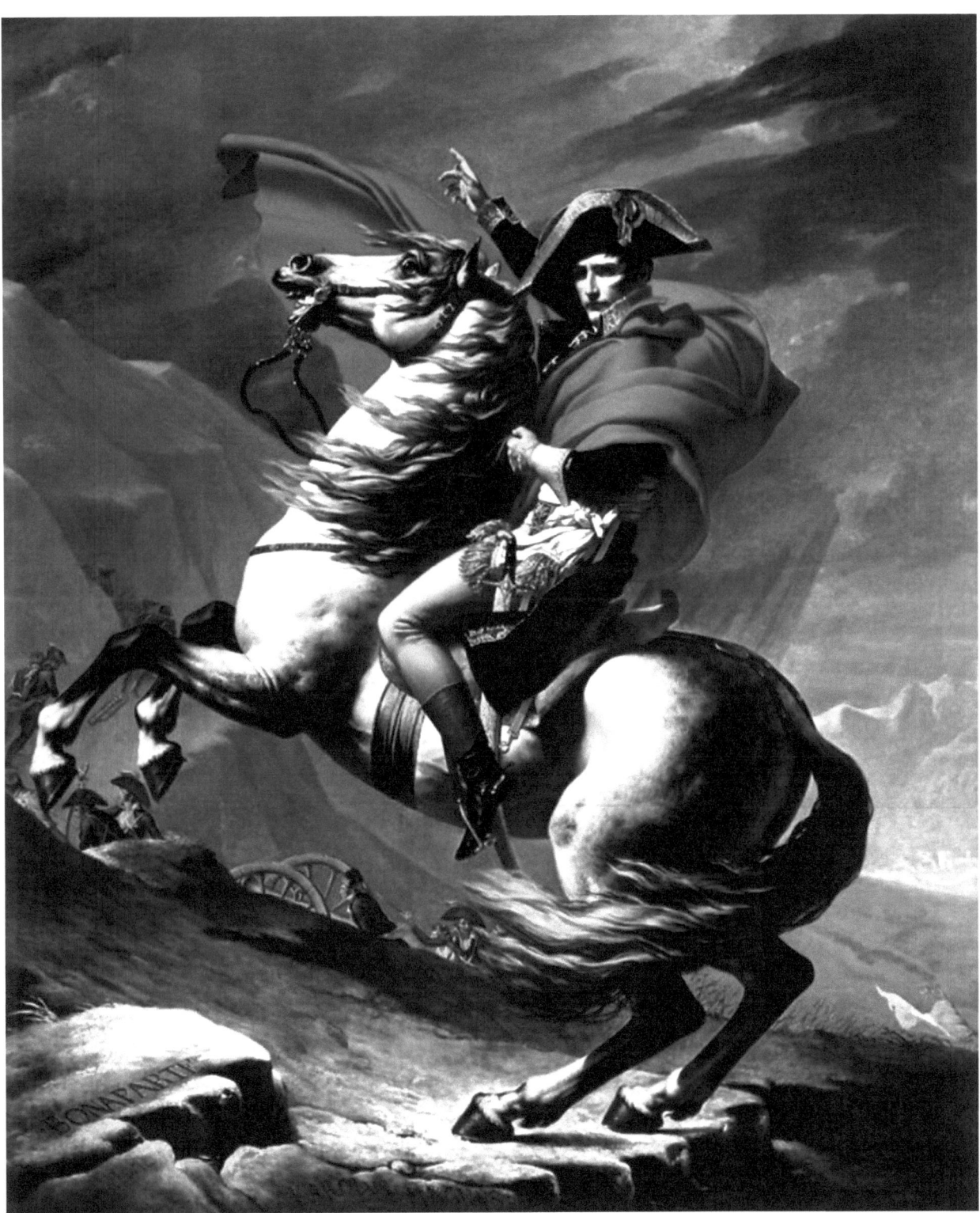

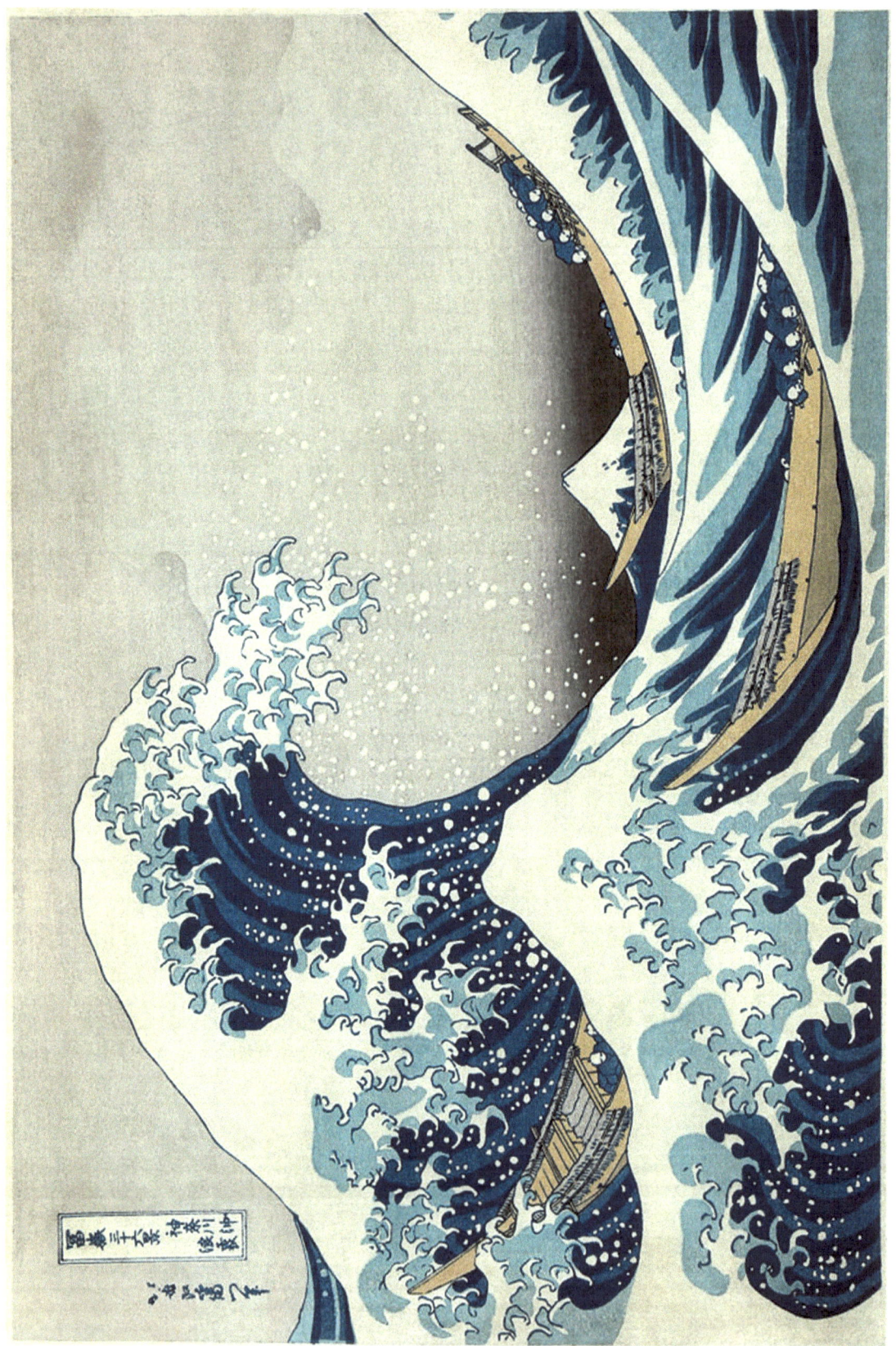

The Great Wave off Kanagawa (c. 1830), Katsushika Hokusai

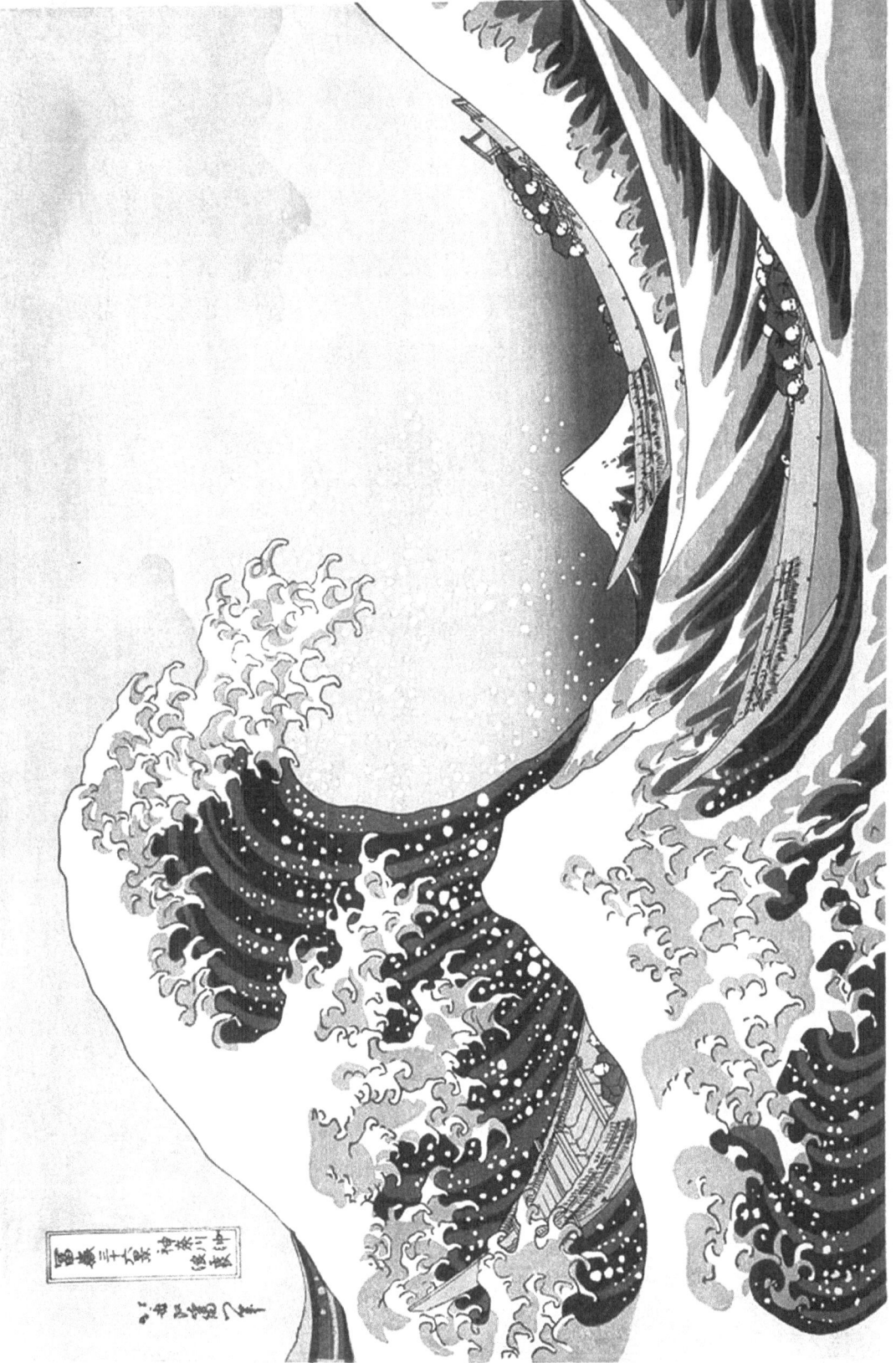

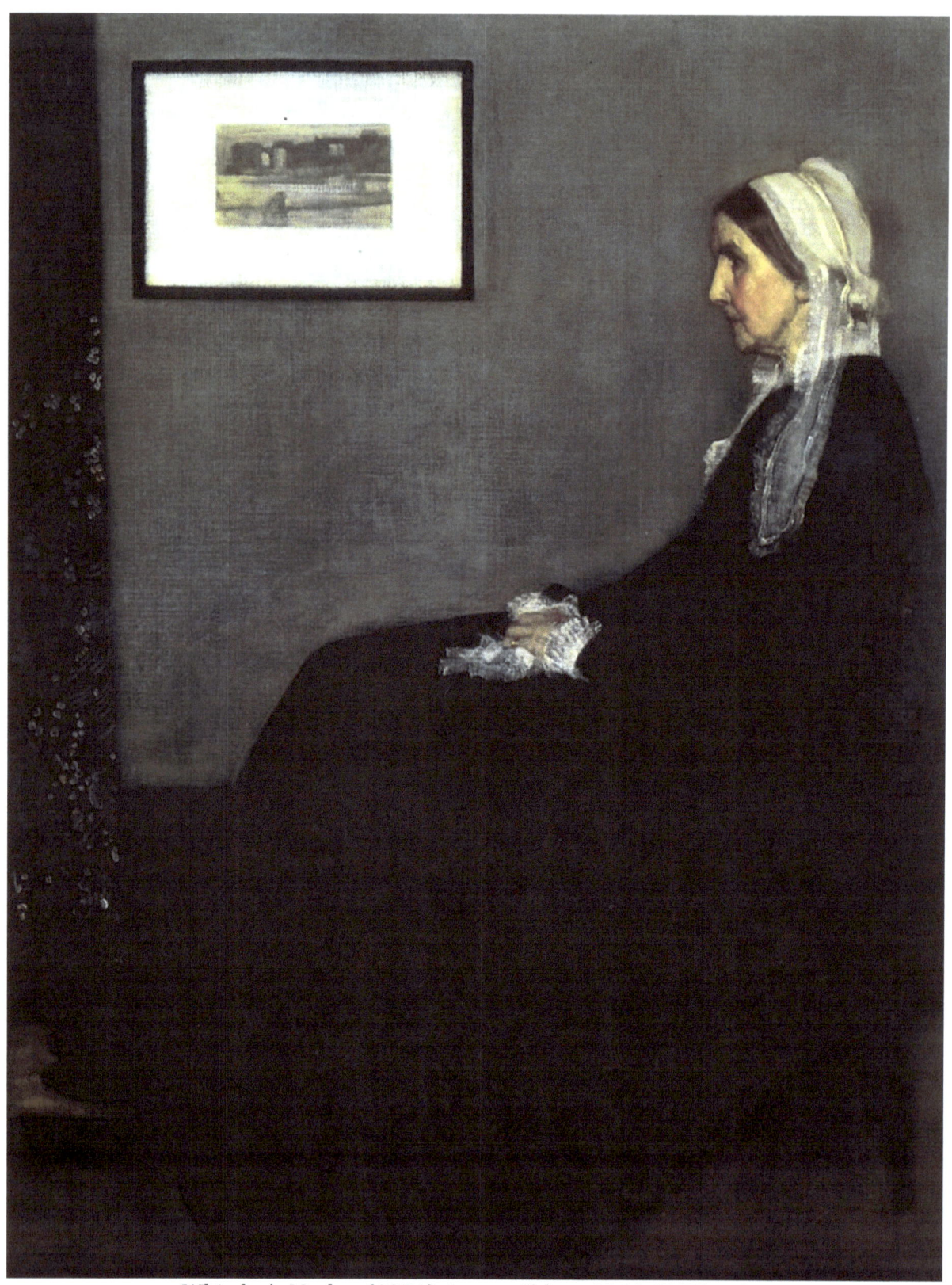

Whistler's Mother (1871), James Abbott McNeill Whistler

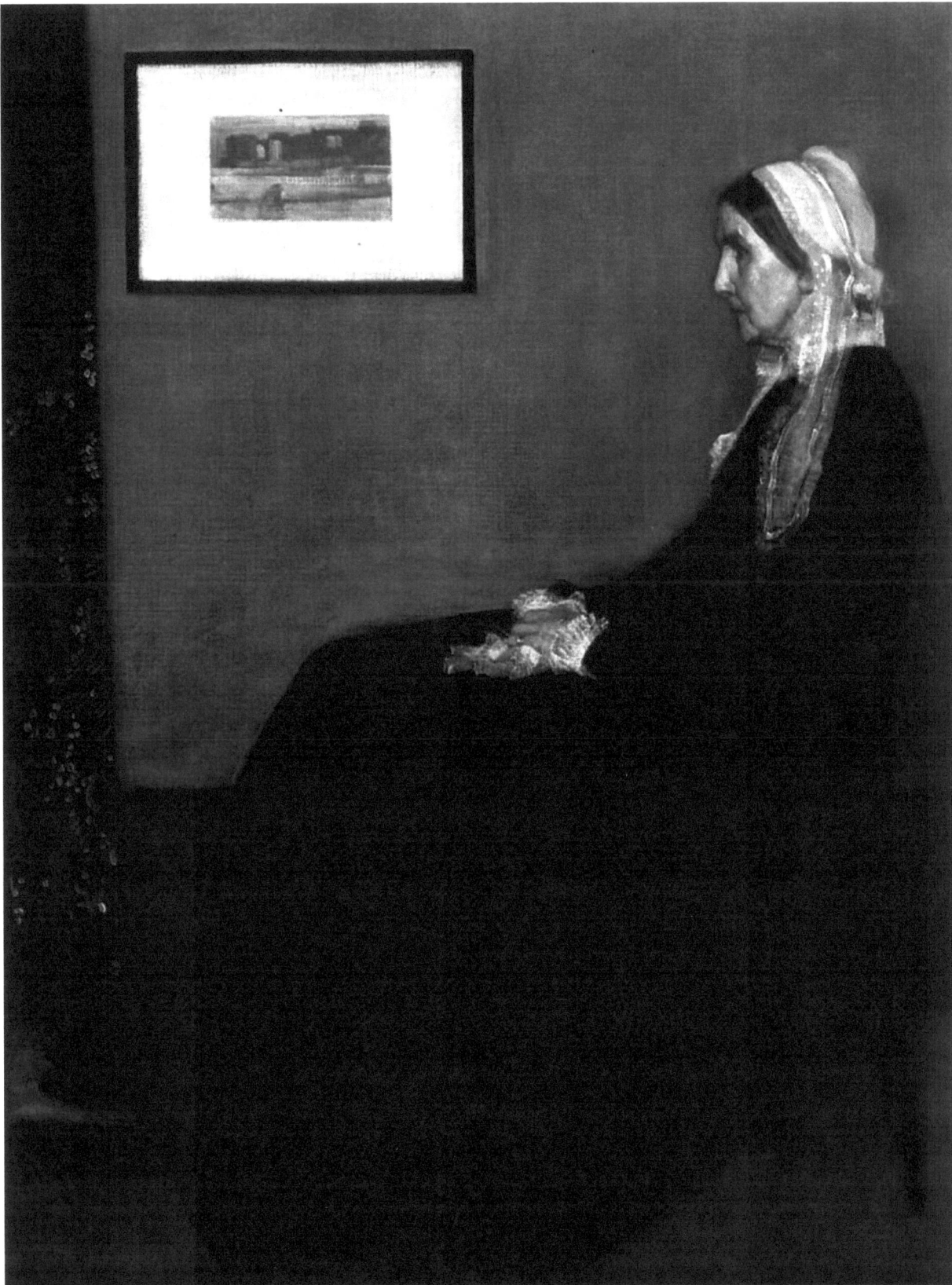

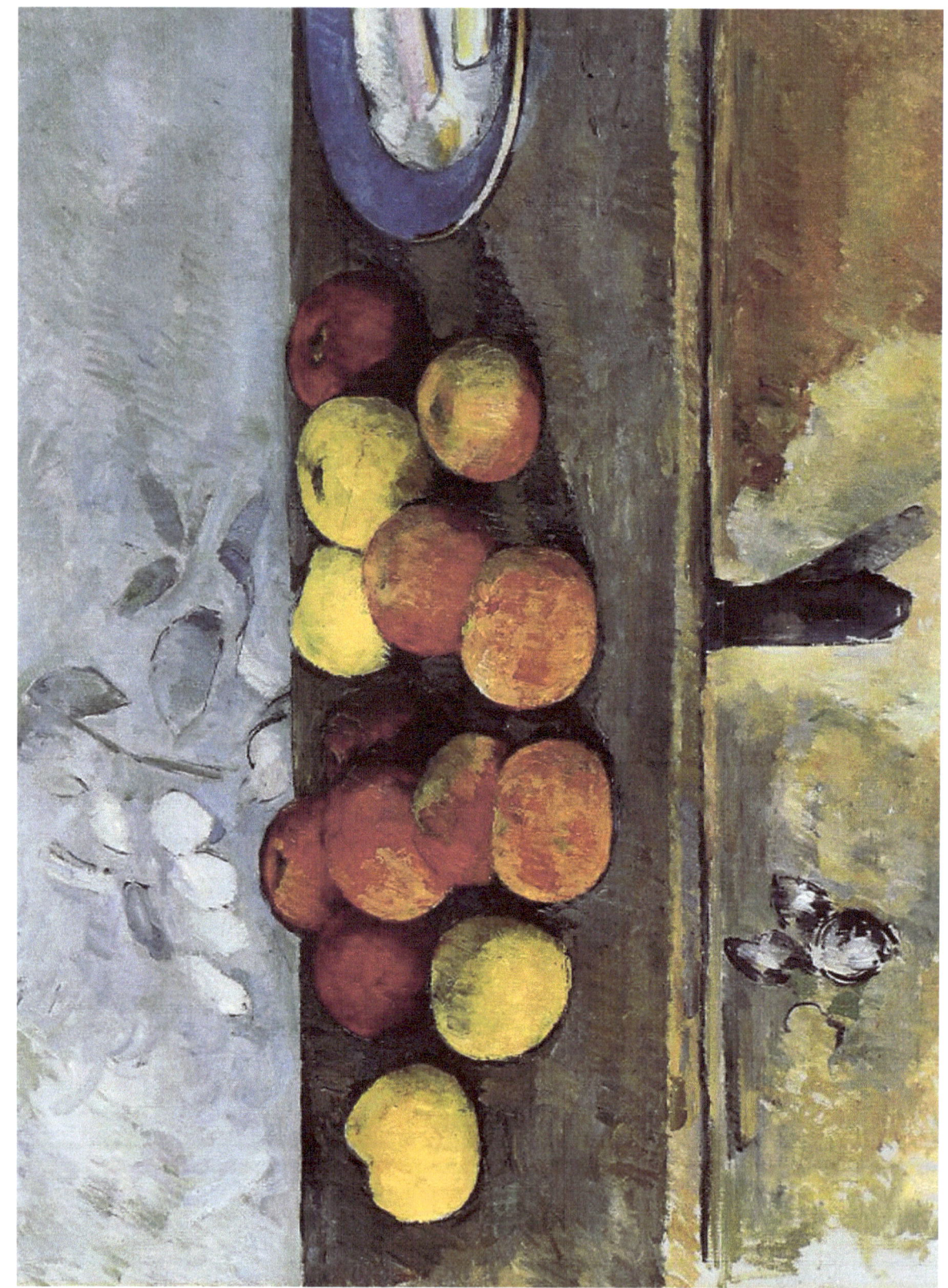

Apples and Biscuits (1880), Paul Cézanne

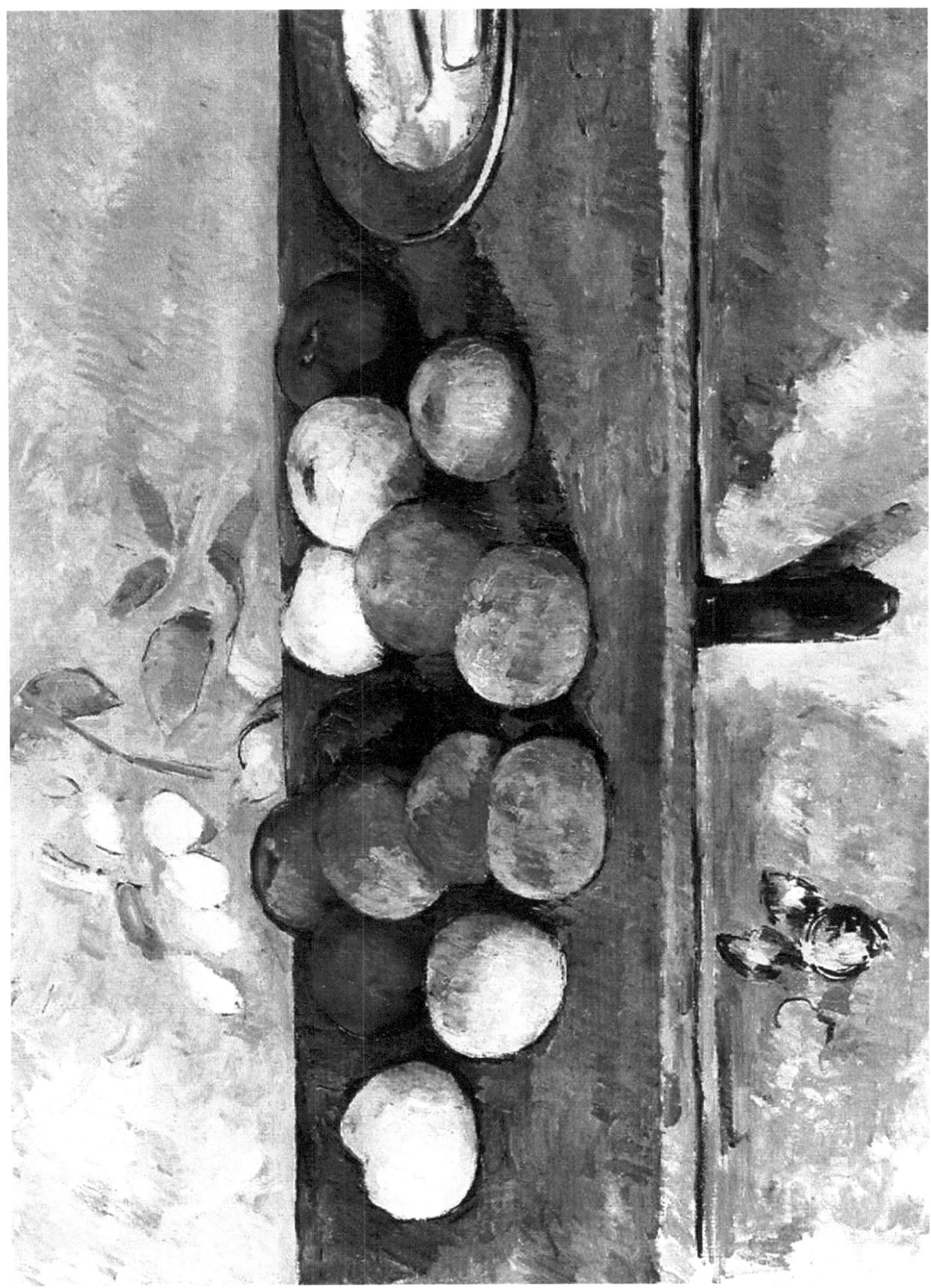

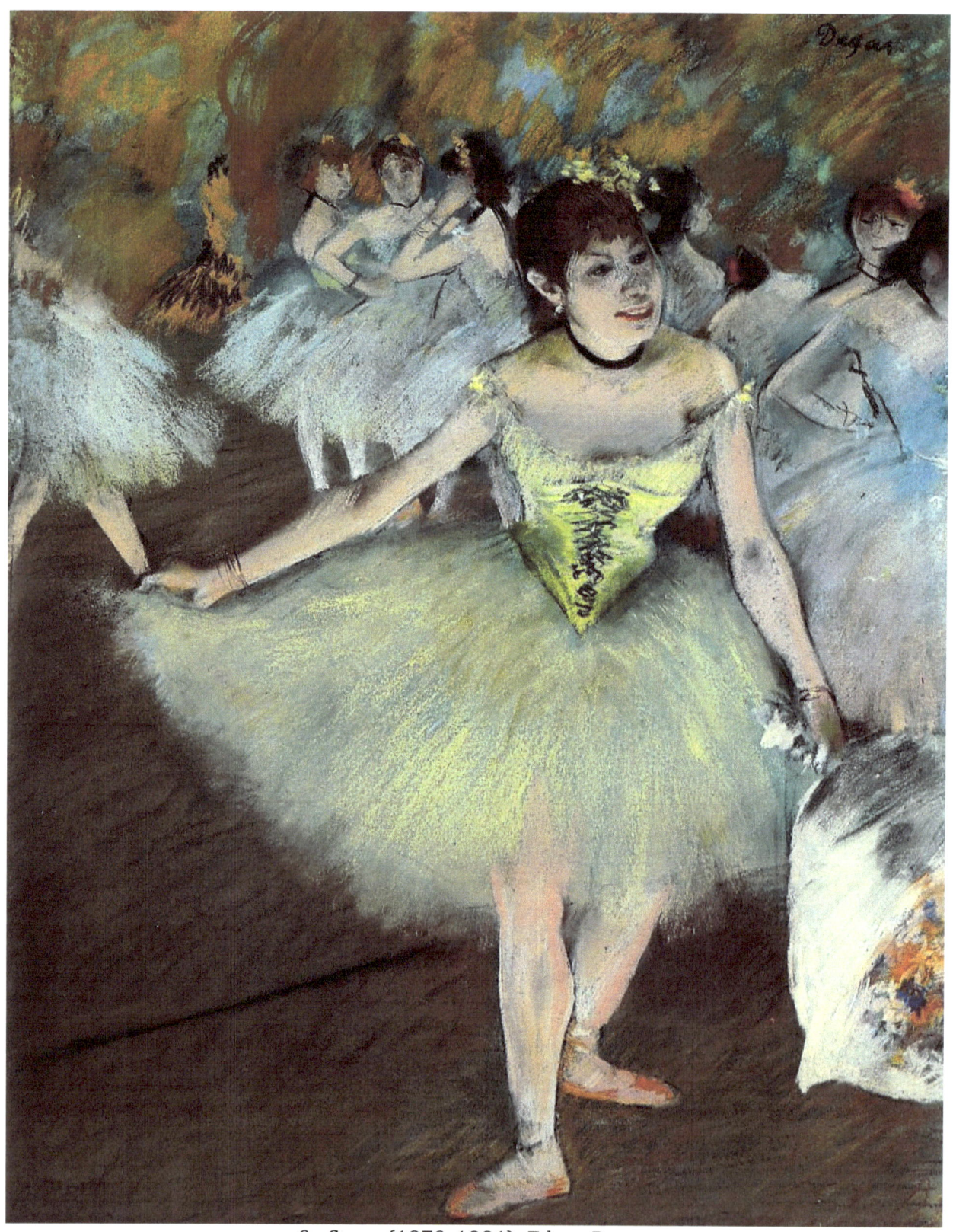

On Stage (1879-1881), Edgar Degas

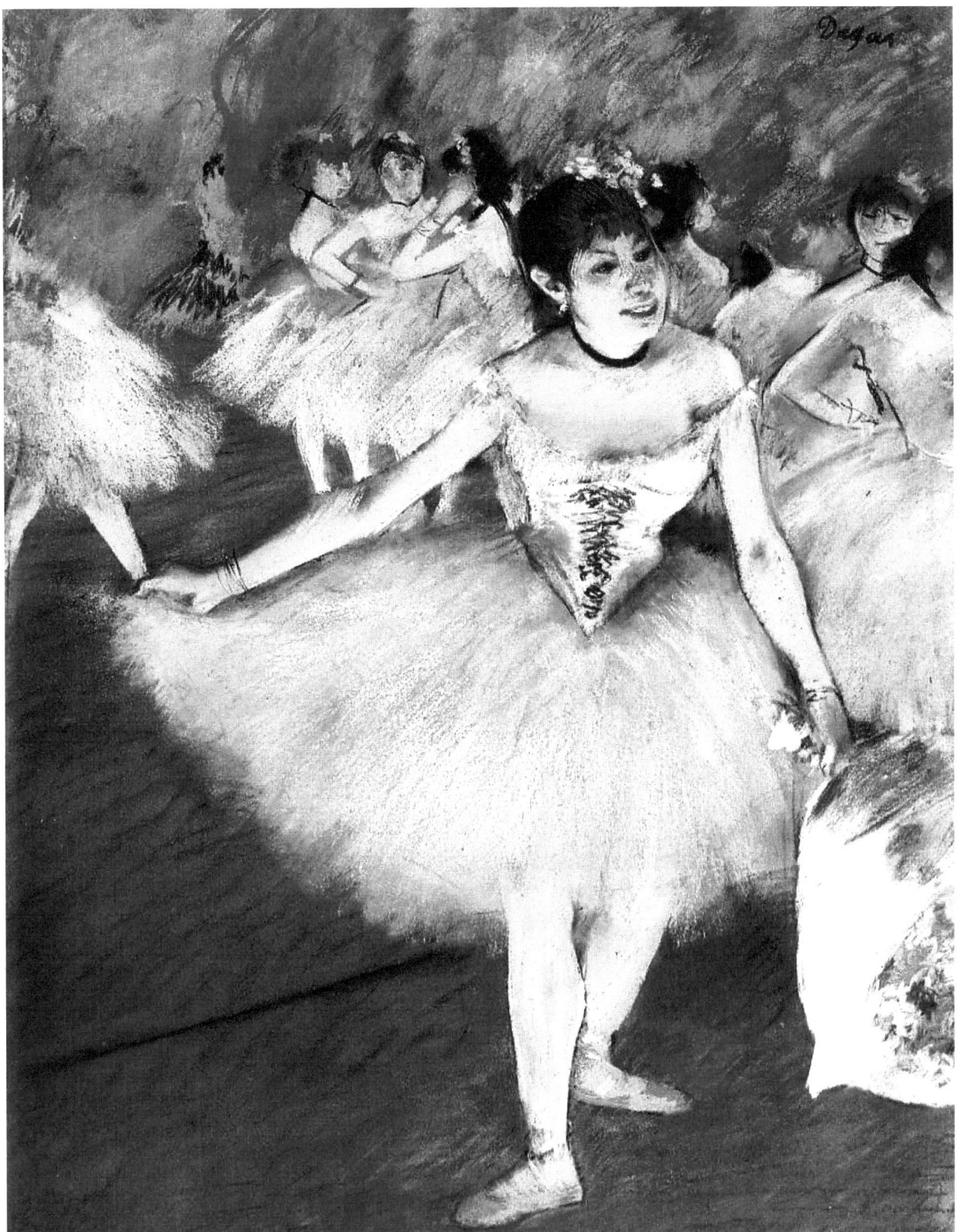

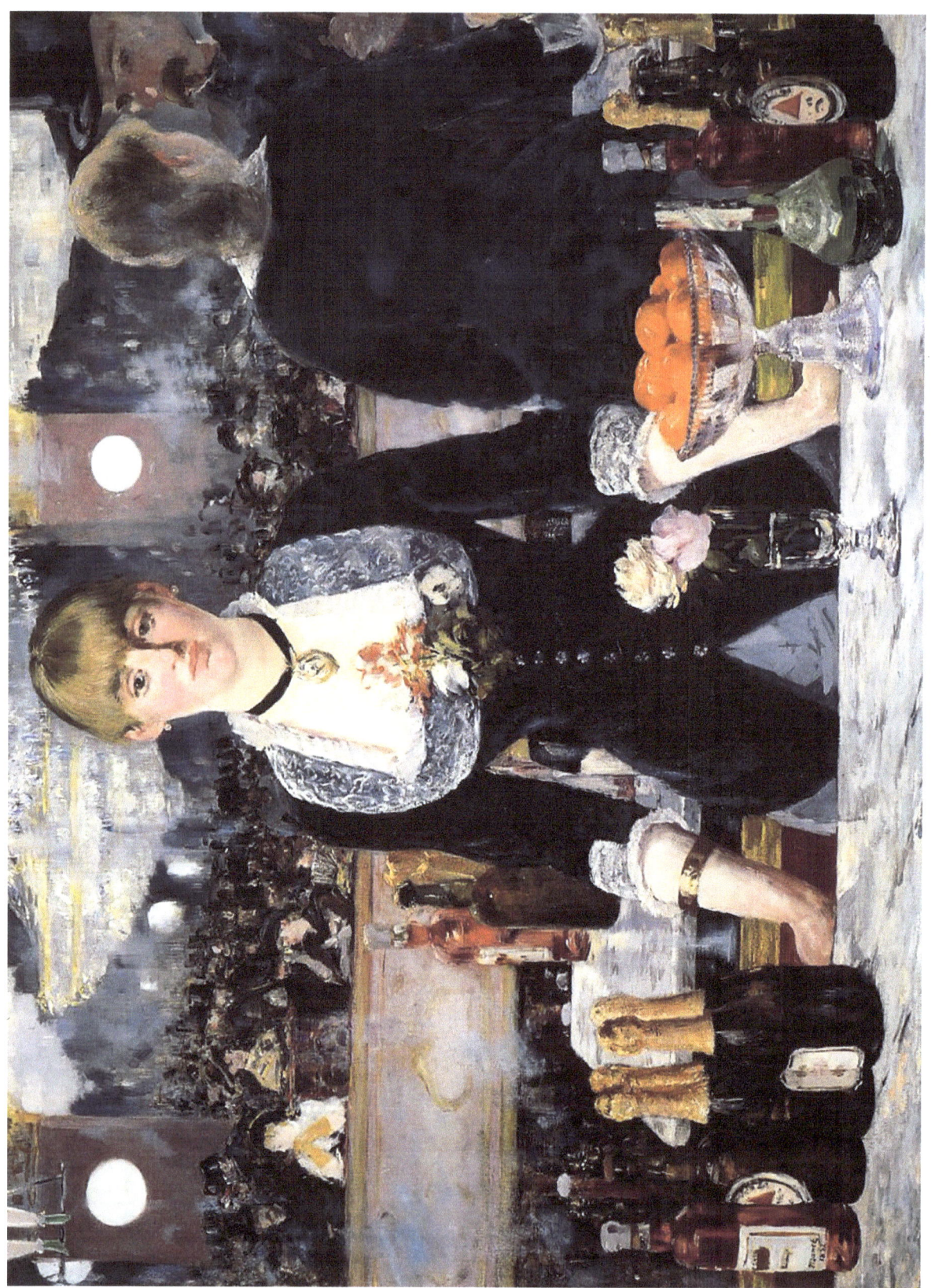

A Bar at the Folies-Bergere (1882), Edouard Manet

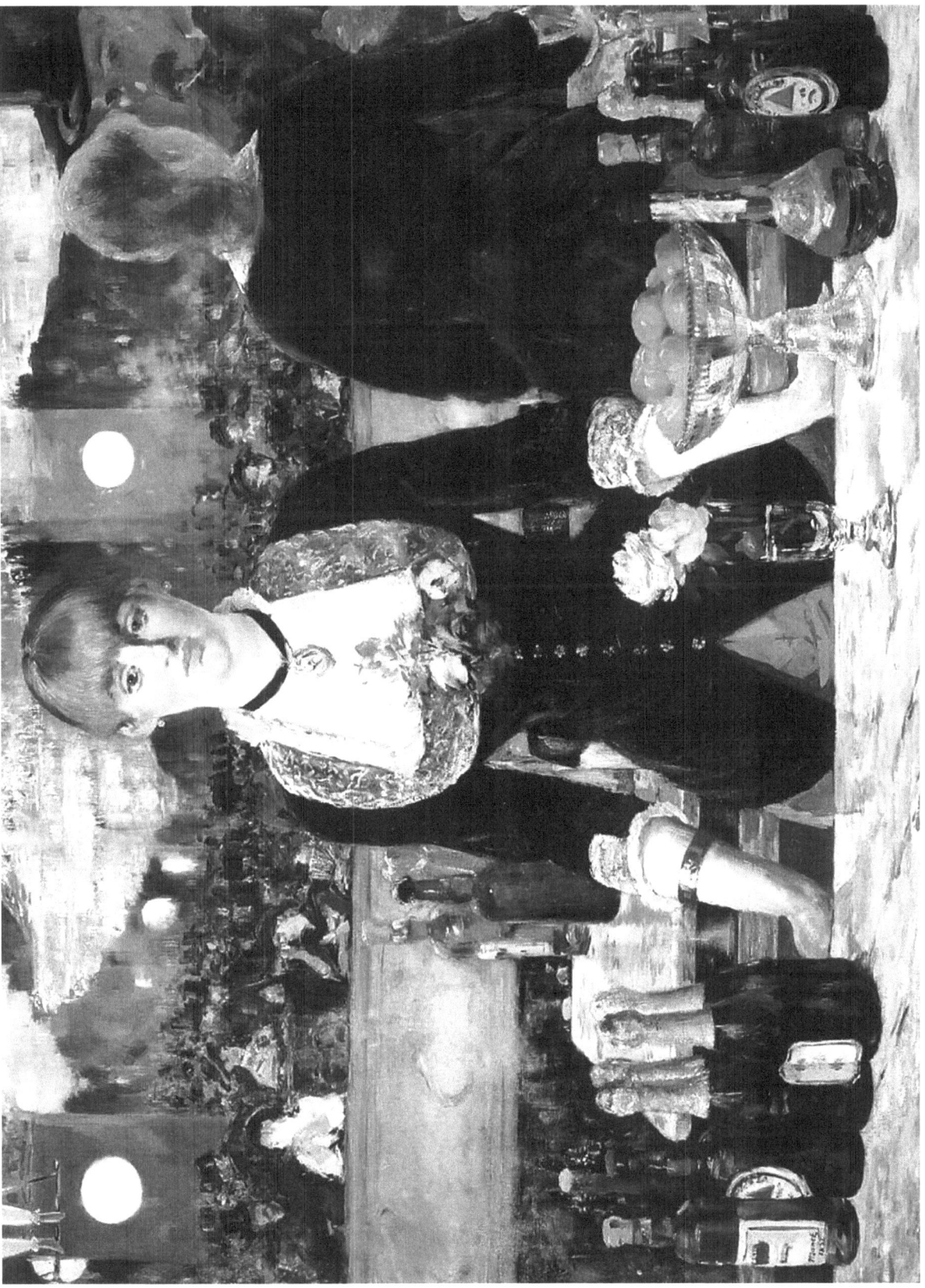

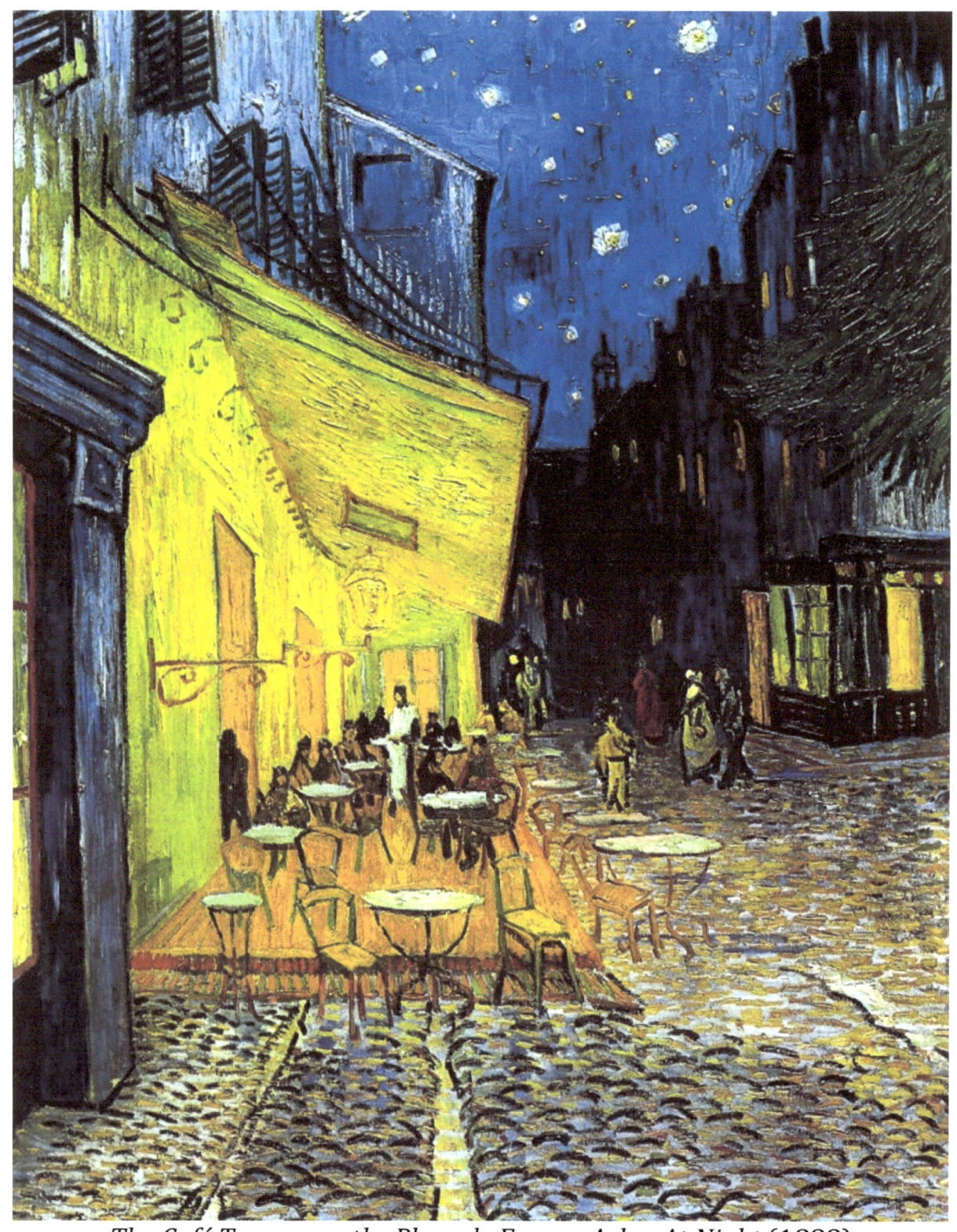

The Café Terrace on the Place de Forum, Arles, At Night (1888)
Vincent van Gogh

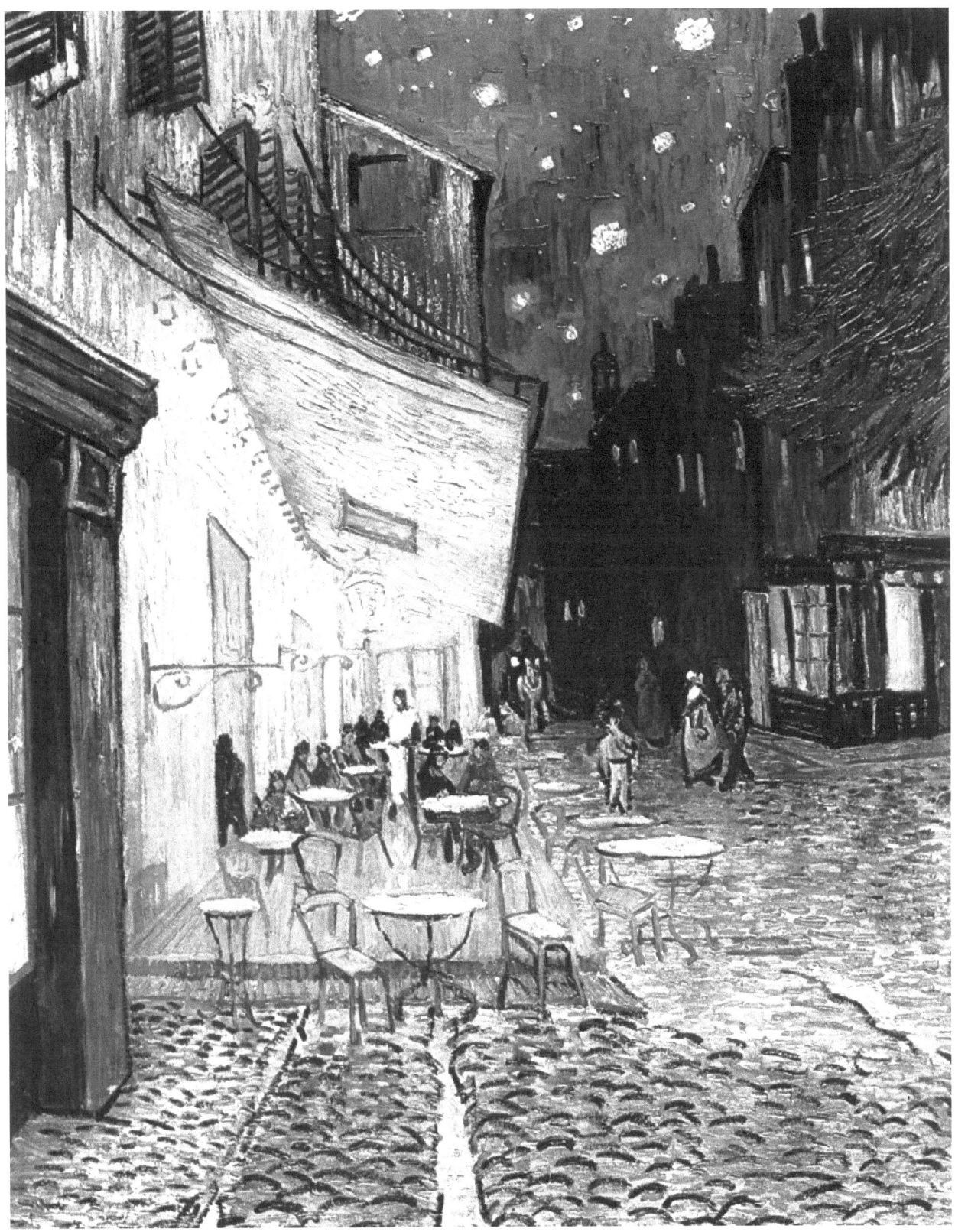

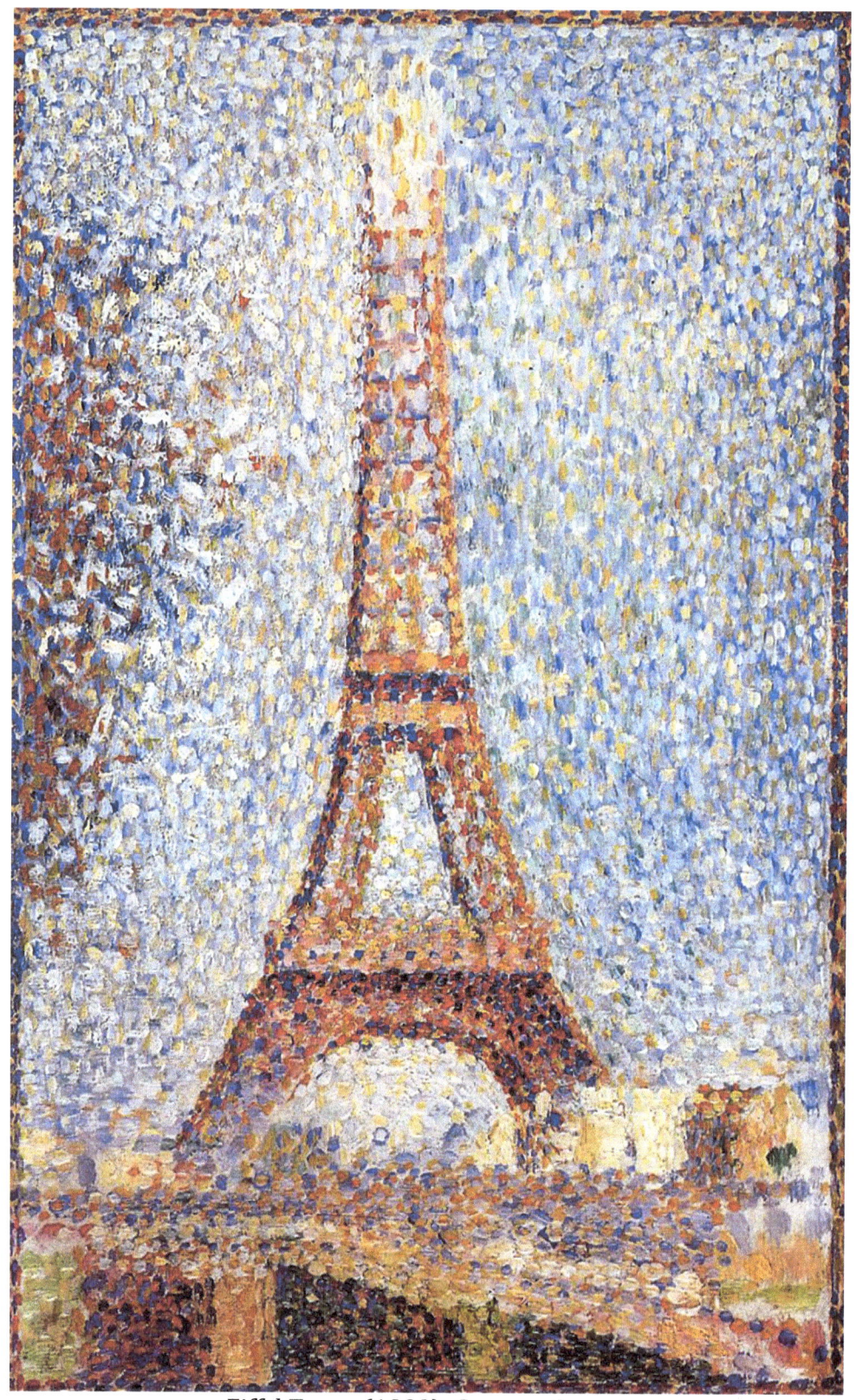

Eiffel Tower (1889), Georges Seurat

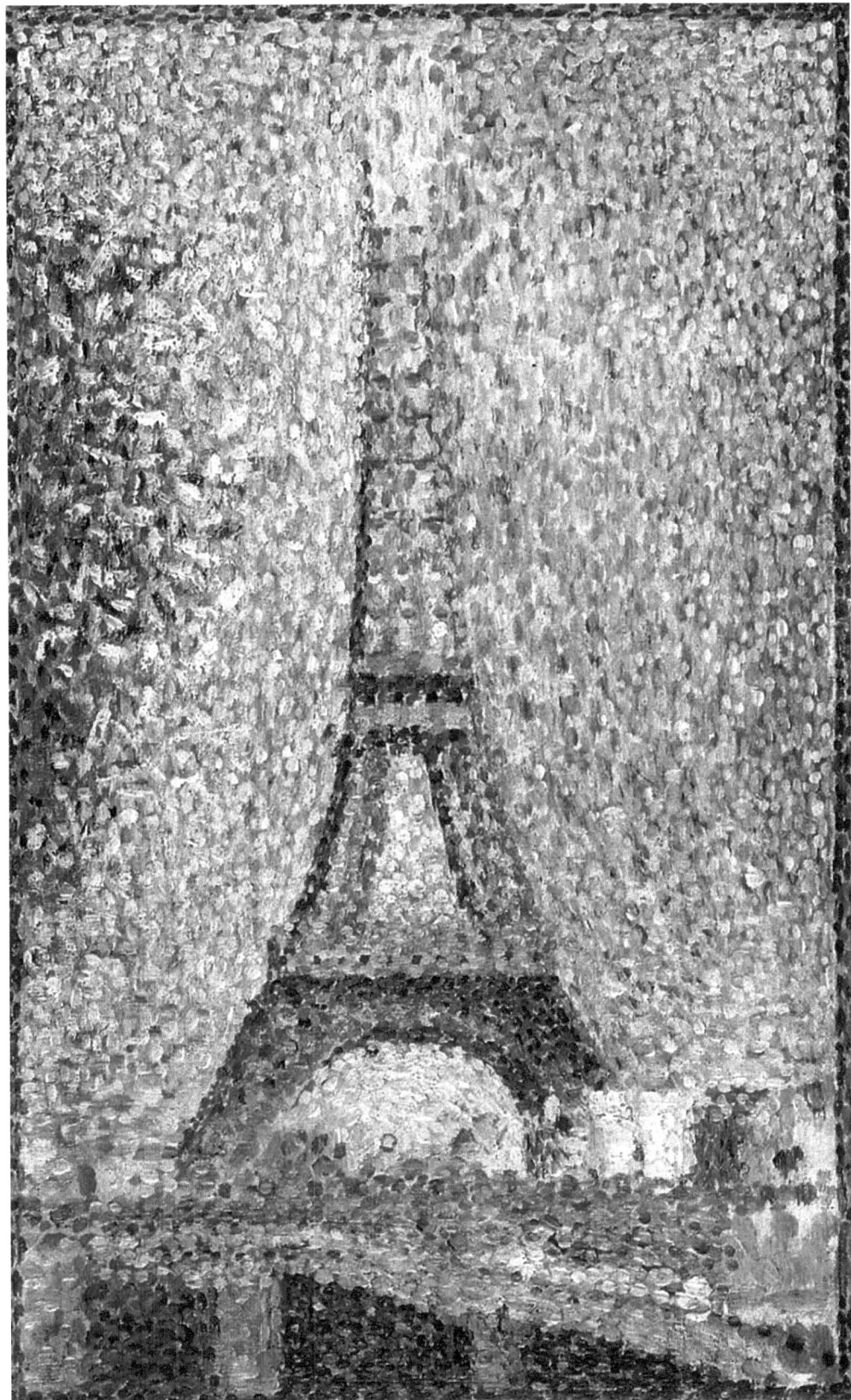

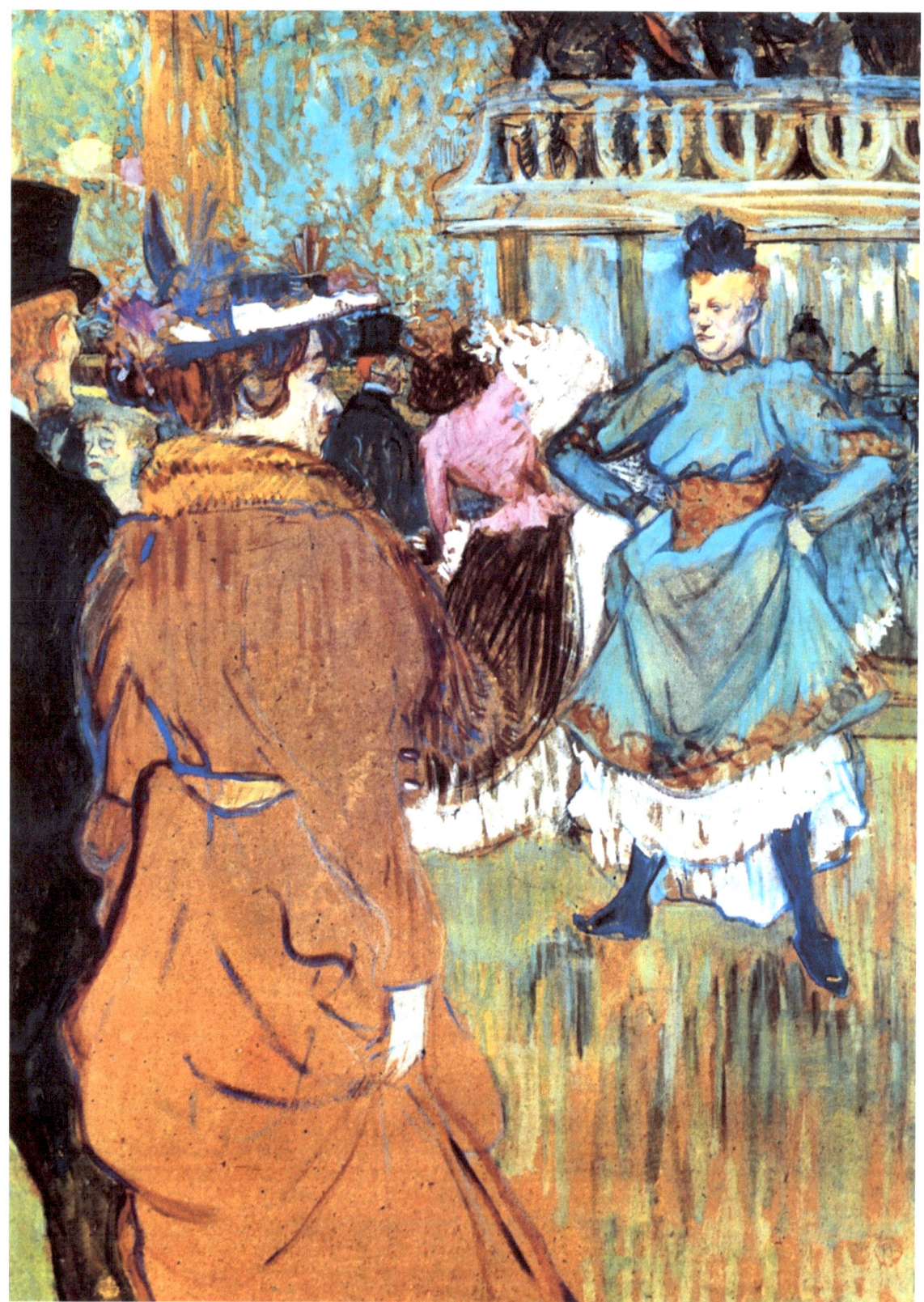

The Beginning of the Quadrille at the Moulin Rouge (1892), Henri de Toulouse-Lautrec

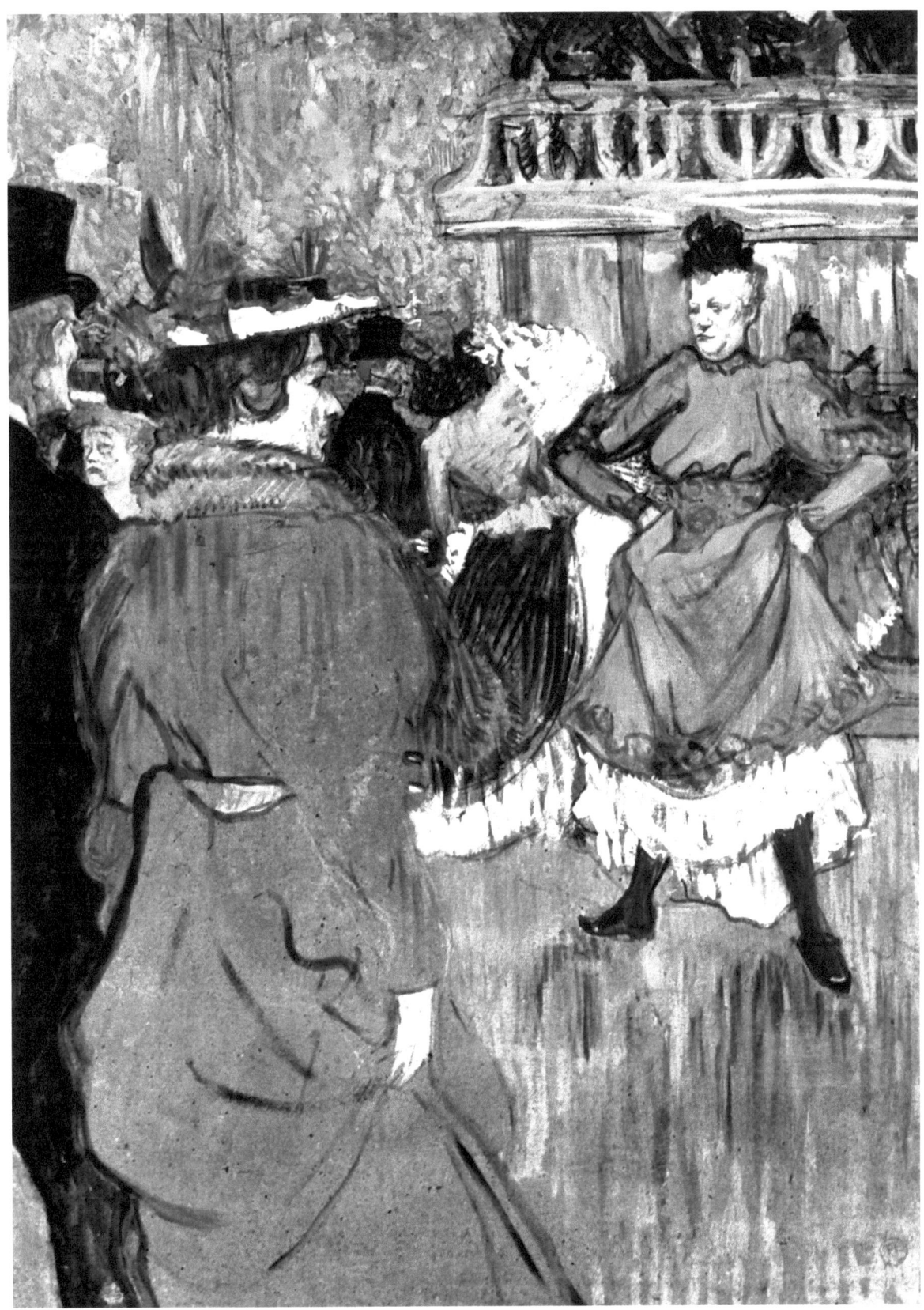

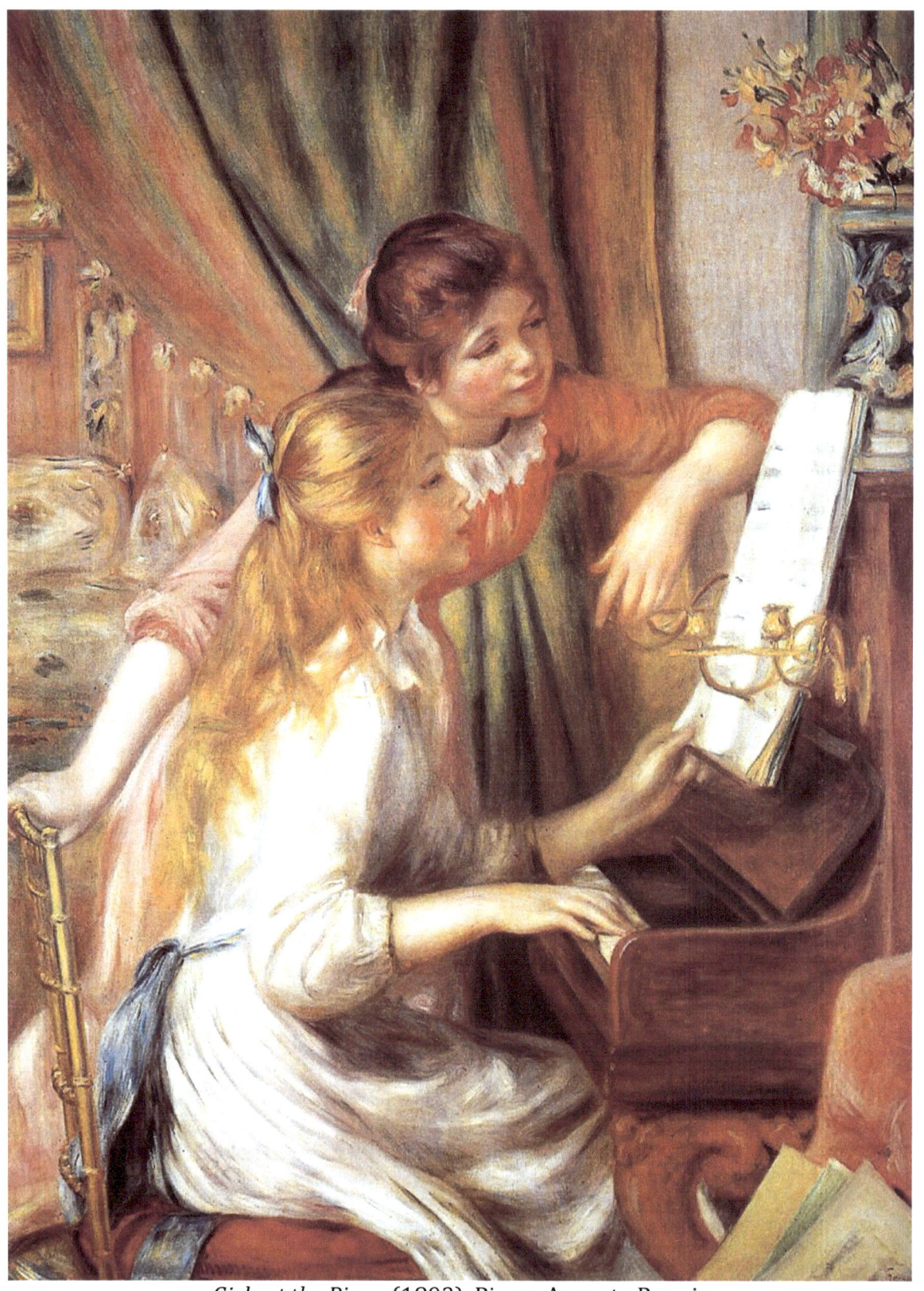

Girls at the Piano (1892), Pierre Auguste Renoir

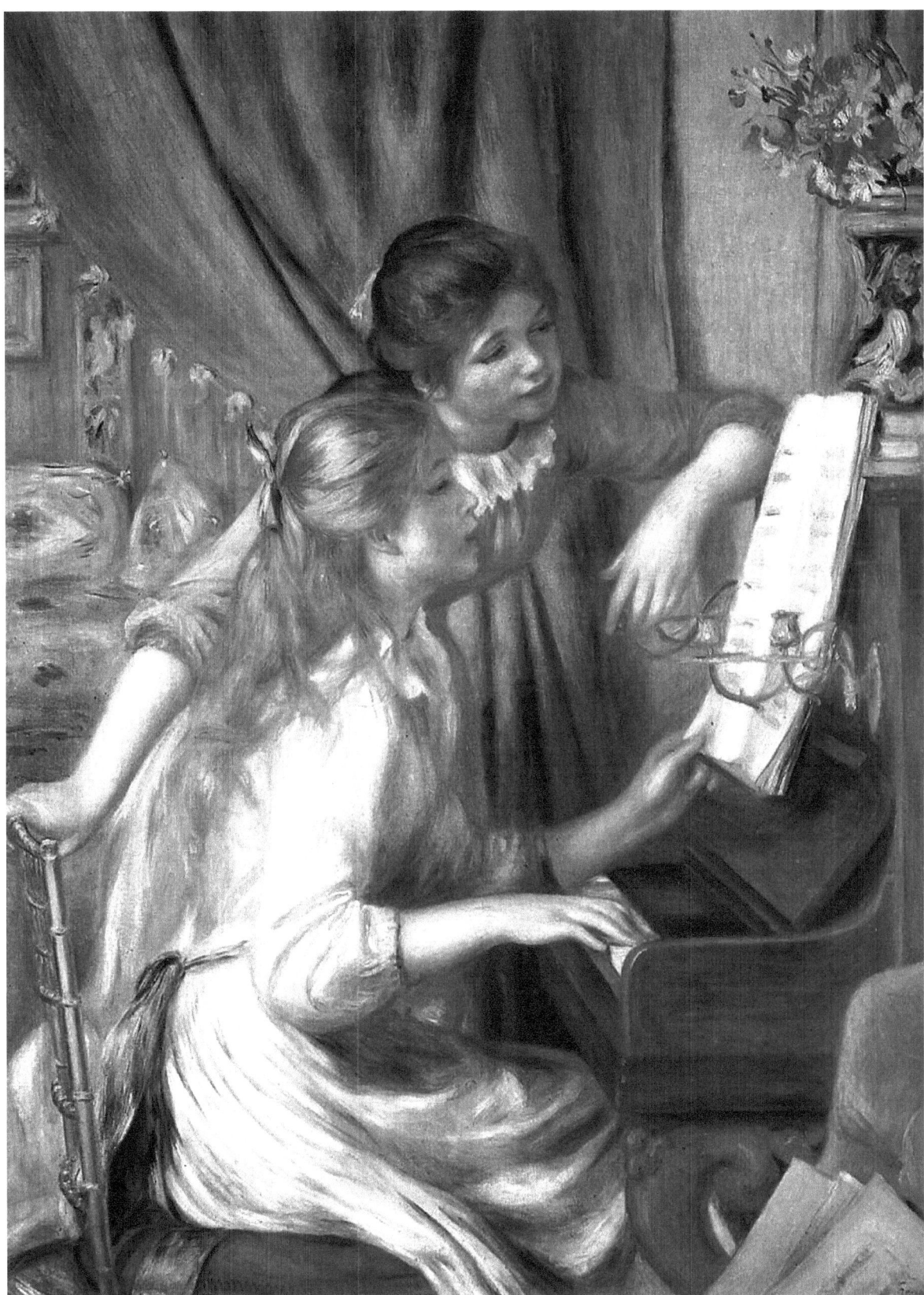

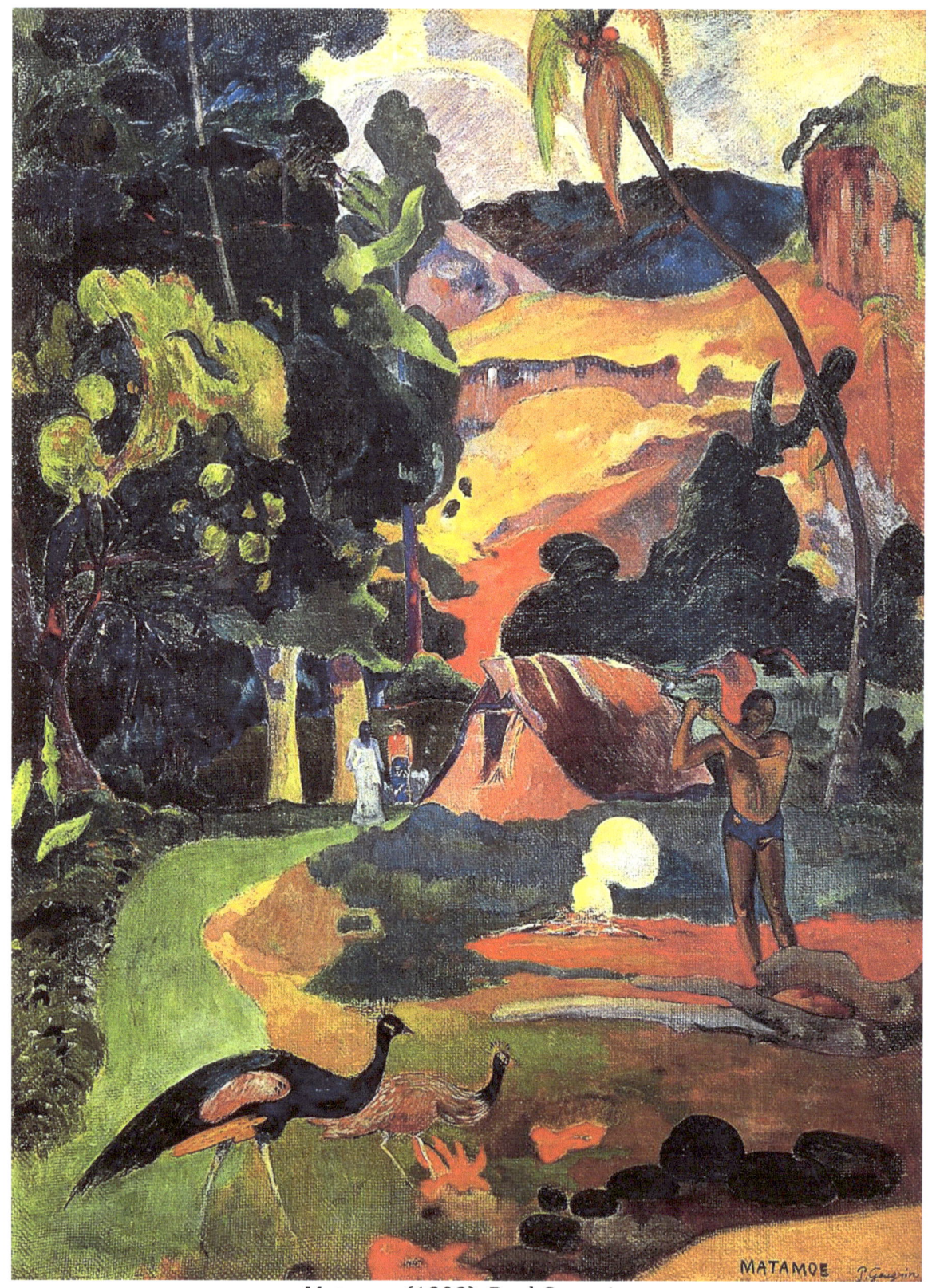

Matamoe (1892), Paul Gauguin

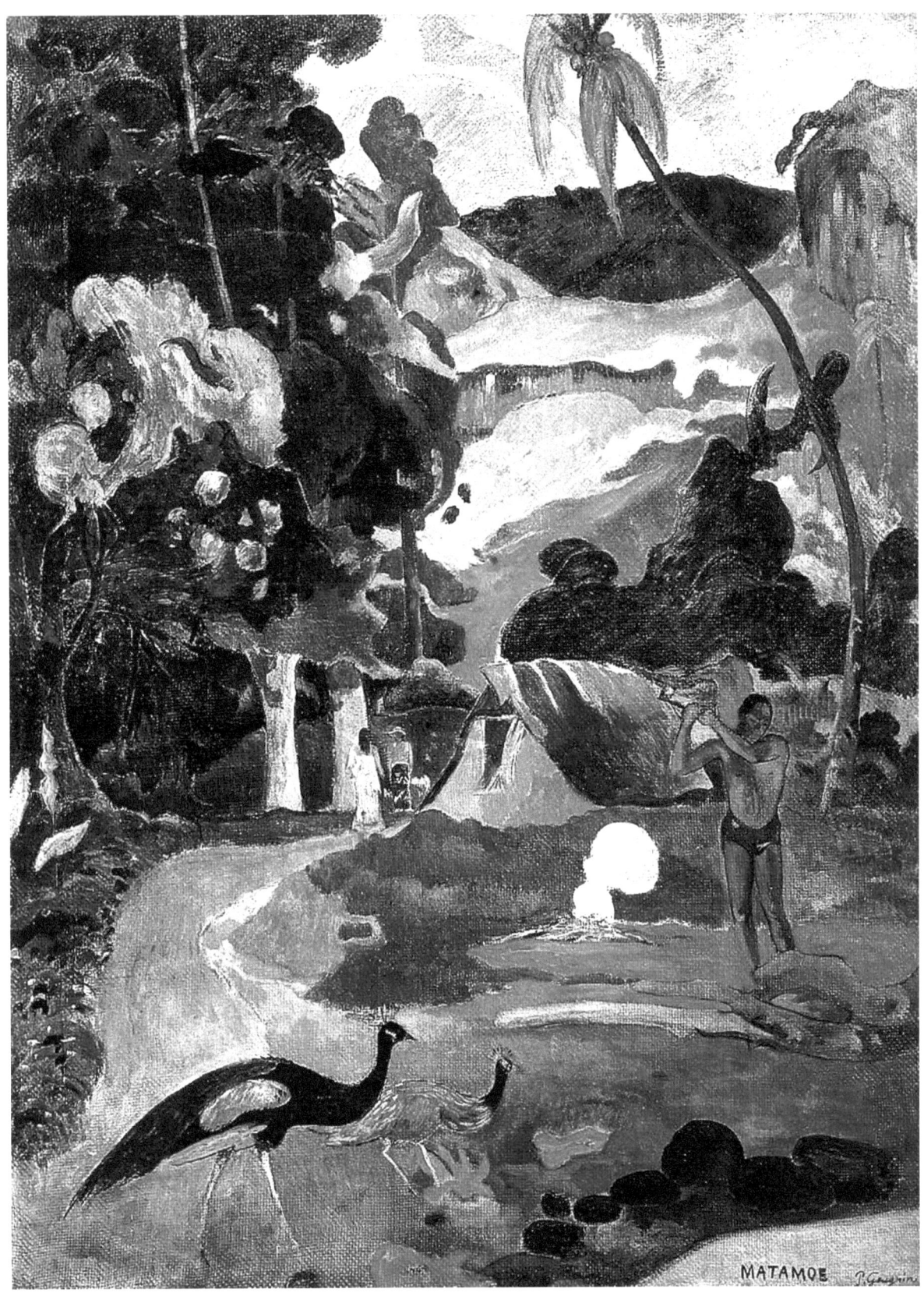

MATAMOE P.Gauguin

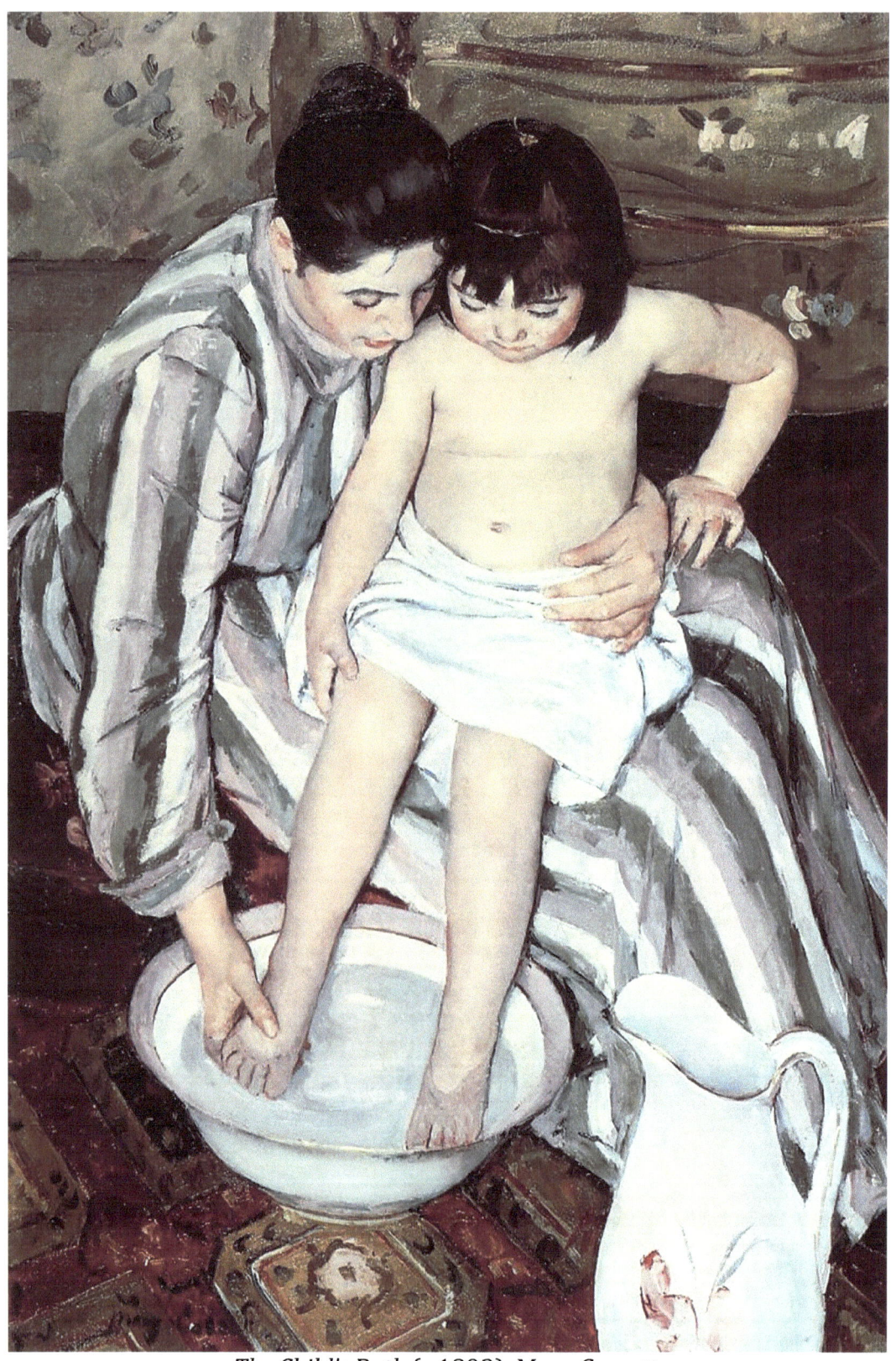

The Child's Bath (c.1893), Mary Cassatt

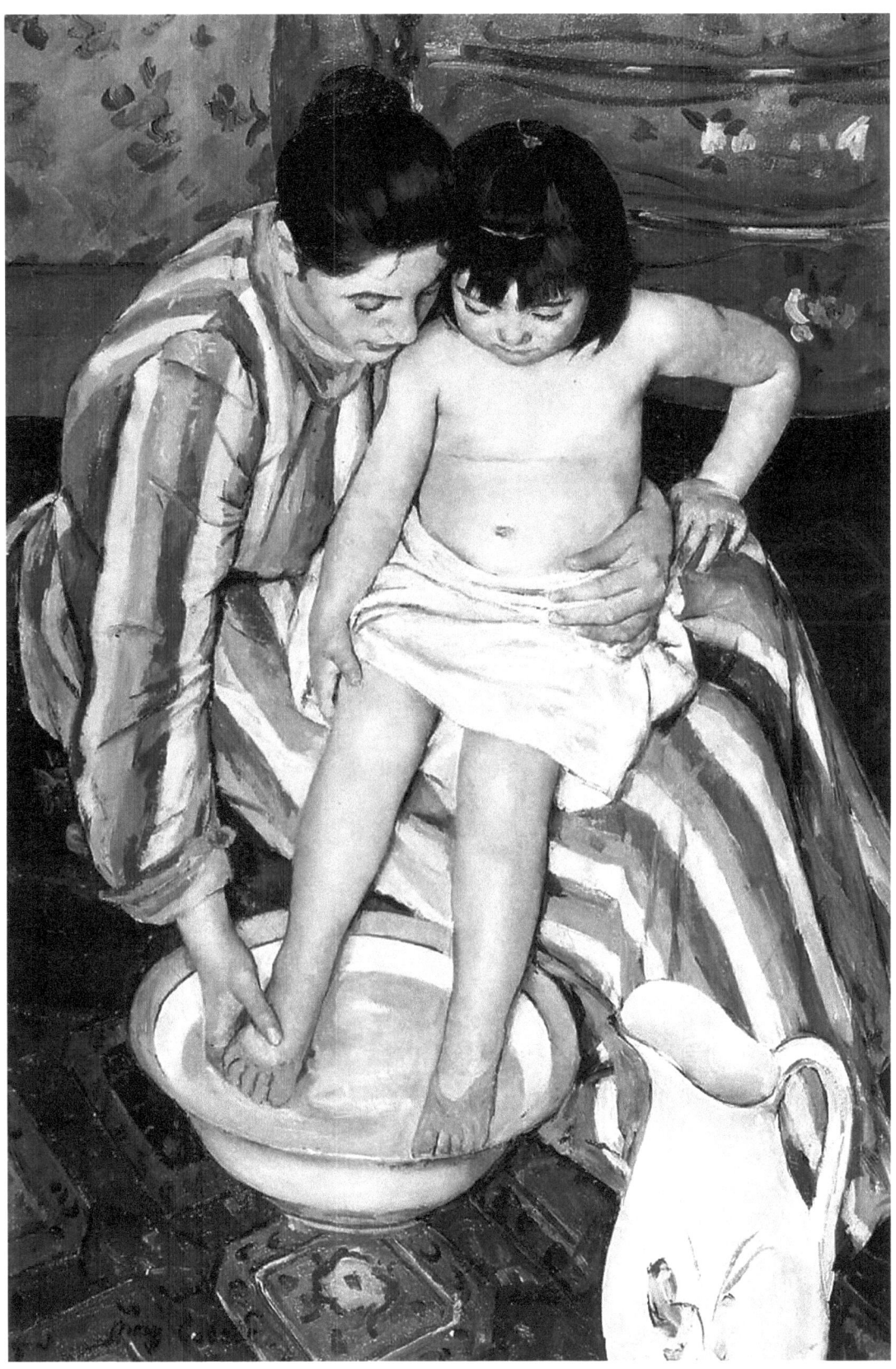

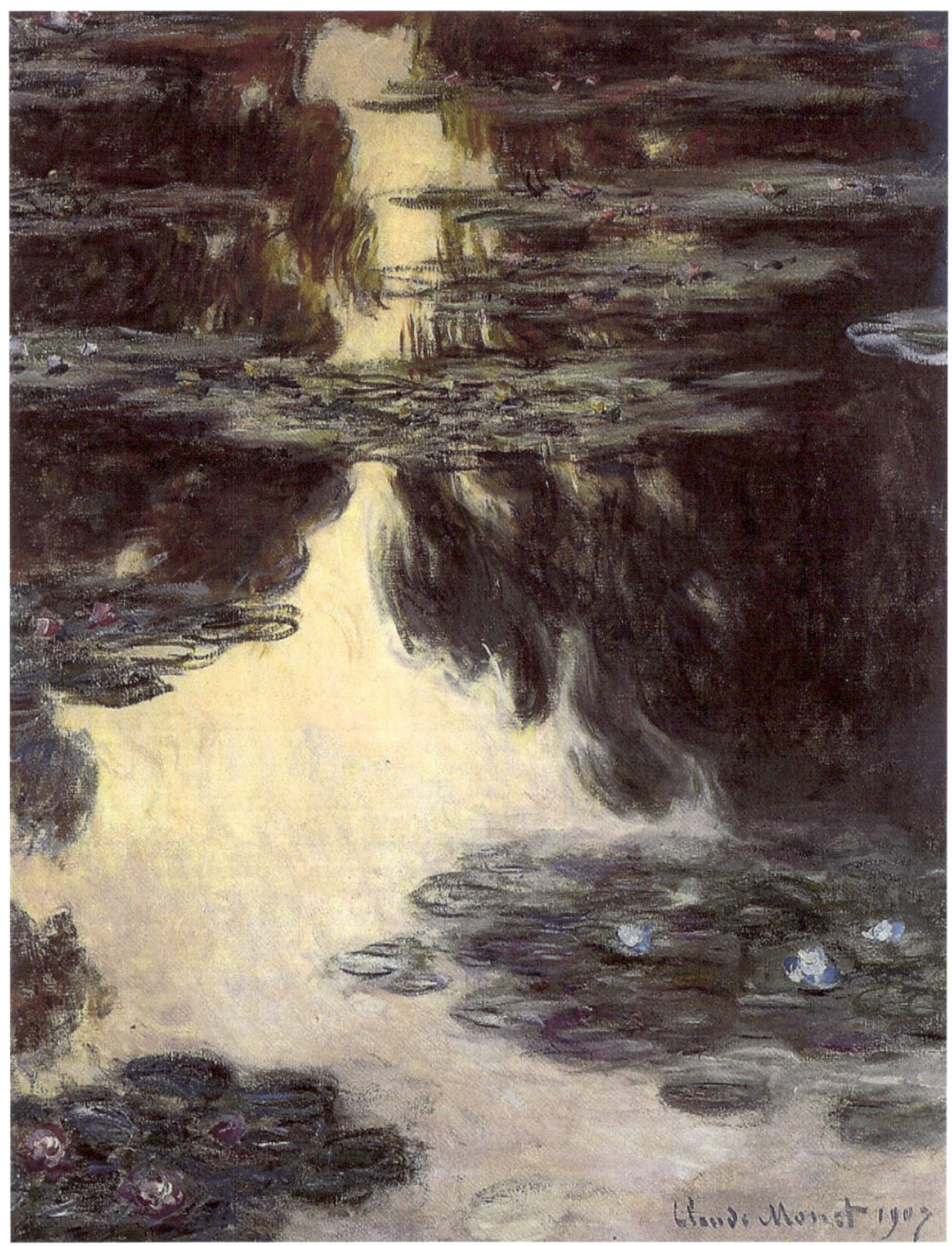

Water-lilies (1907), Claude Monet

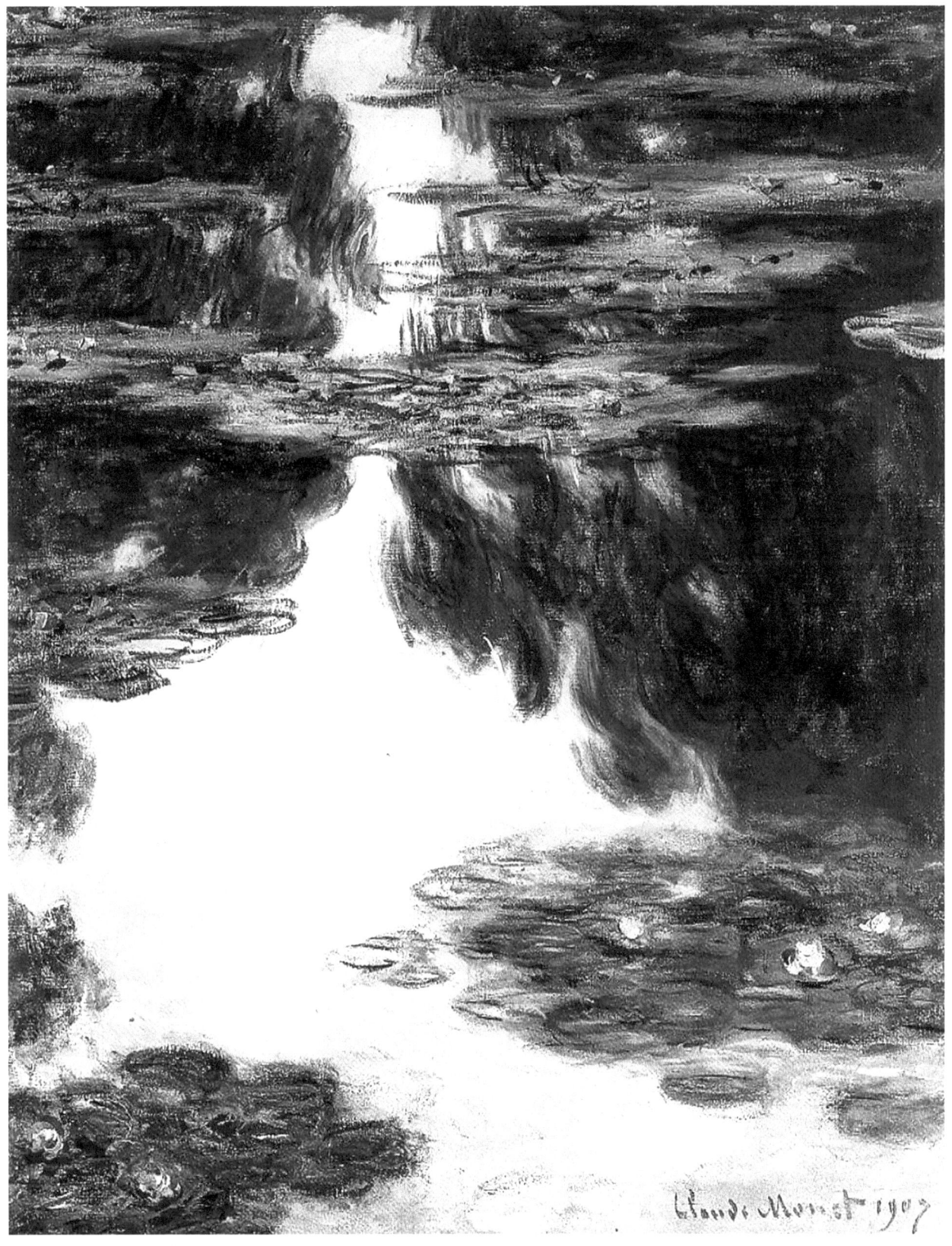

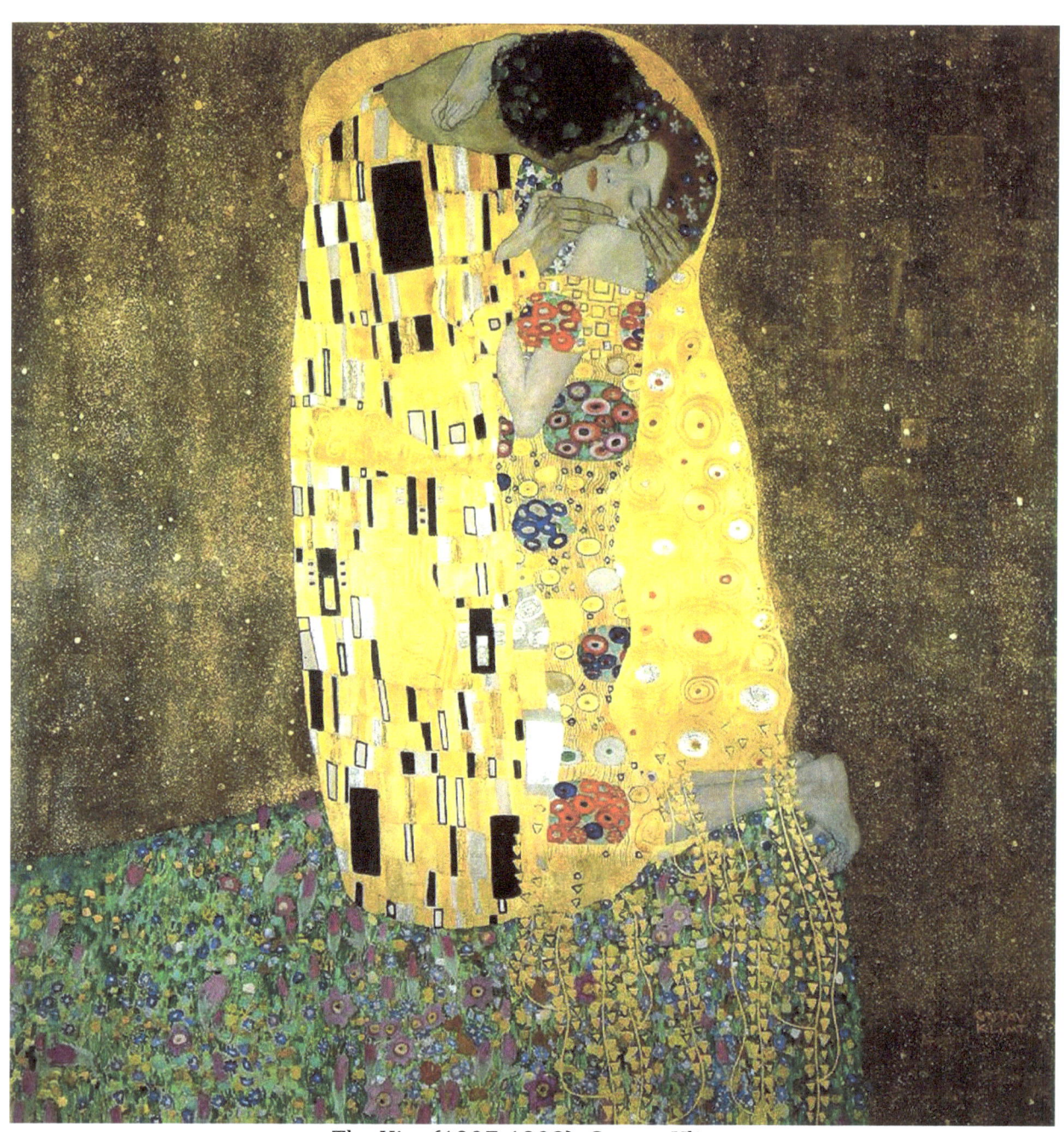

The Kiss (1907-1908), Gustav Klimt

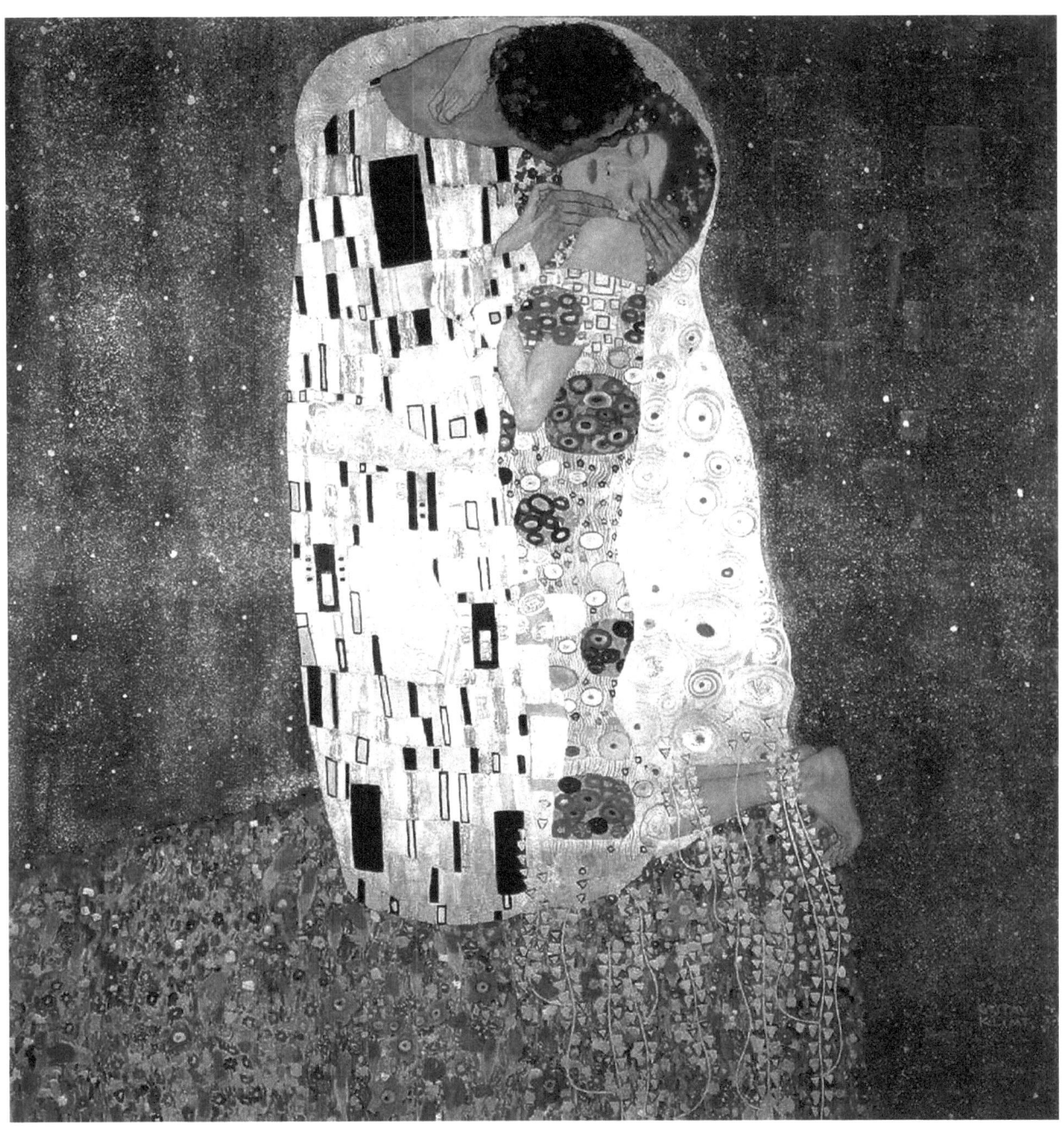

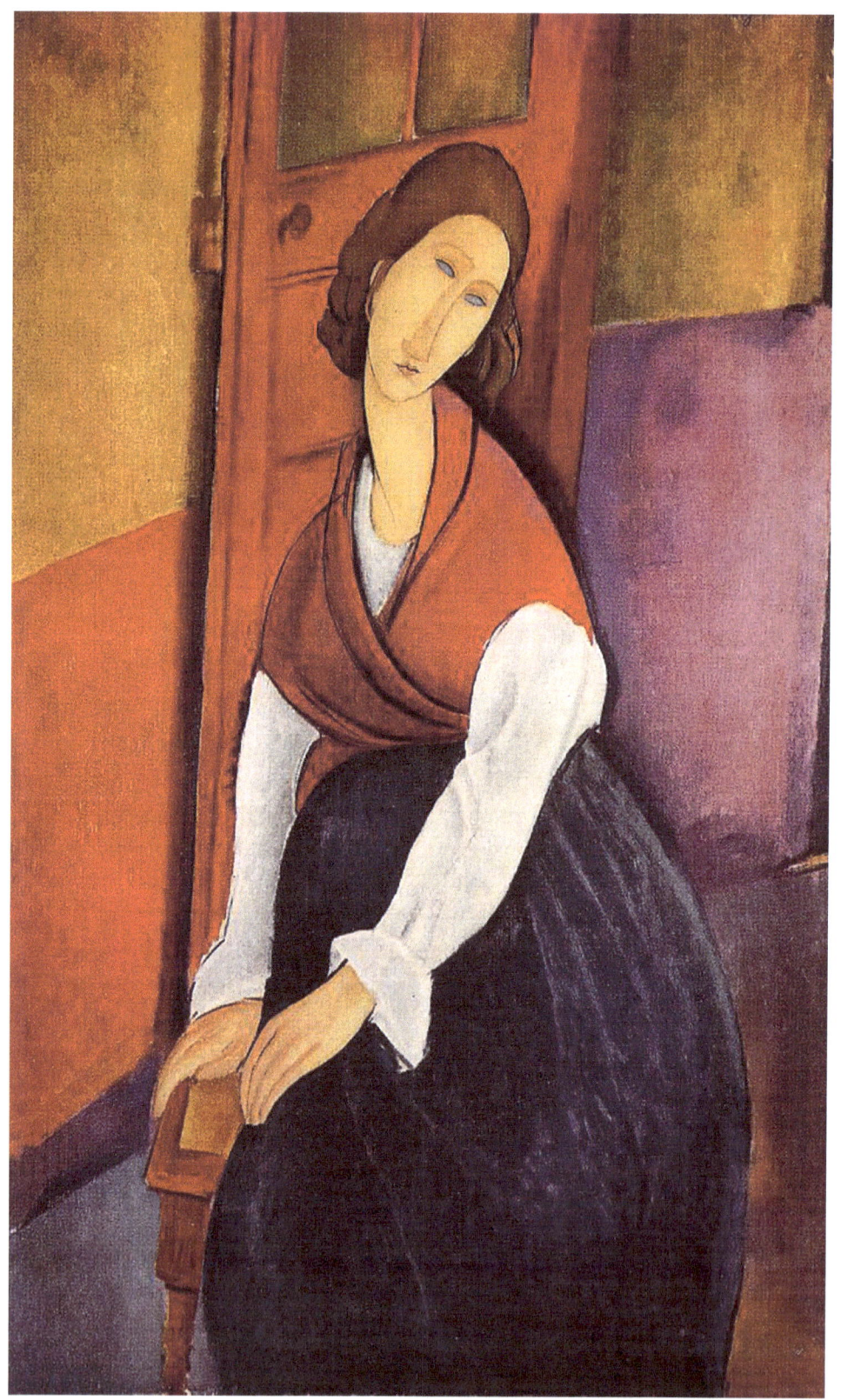

Jeanne Hebuterne (1919), Amedeo Modigliani

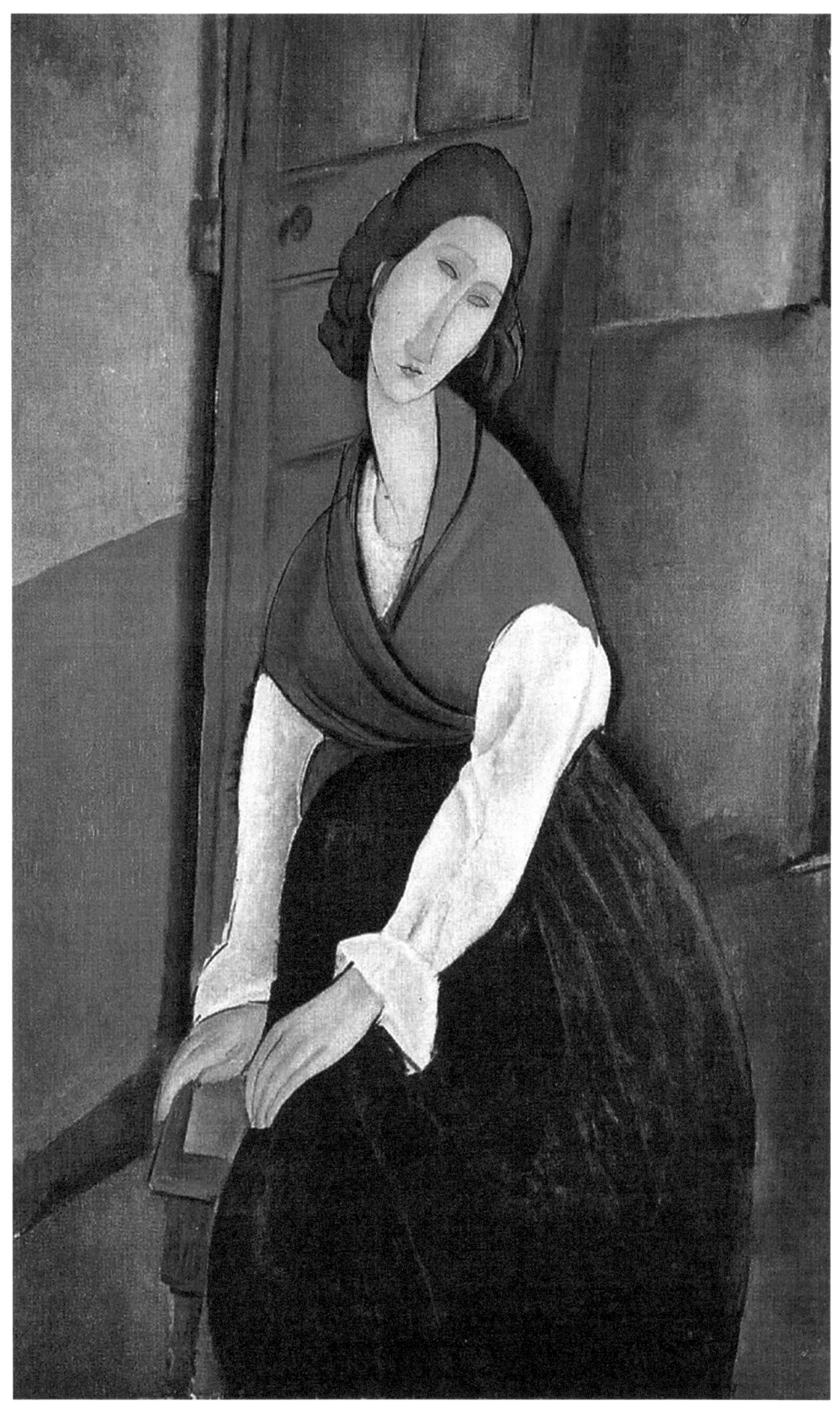

www.ingramcontent.com/pod-product-compliance
Lightning Source LLC
Chambersburg PA
CBHW051055180526
45172CB00002B/649